SURVIVING
THE
PERFECT
STORM

HOW TO CREATE A FINANCIAL
PLAN THAT WILL WITHSTAND ANY CRISIS

MICHAEL CANET, JD LLM

Published by Advantage, Charleston, South Carolina.
Member of Advantage Media Group.

ADVANTAGE is a registered trademark and the Advantage colophon is a trademark of Advantage Media Group, Inc.

Printed in the United States of America.

ISBN: 978-159932-308-4
LCCN: 2012937141

This publication is designed to provide accurate and authoritative information in regard to the subject matter covered. It is sold with the understanding that the publisher is not engaged in rendering legal, accounting, or other professional services. If legal advice or other expert assistance is required, the services of a competent professional person should be sought.

Advantage Media Group is proud to be a part of the Tree Neutral® program. Tree Neutral offsets the number of trees consumed in the production and printing of this book by taking proactive steps such as planting trees in direct proportion to the number of trees used to print books. To learn more about Tree Neutral, please visit **www.treeneutral.com**. To learn more about Advantage's commitment to being a responsible steward of the environment, please visit **www.advantagefamily.com/green**

Advantage Media Group is a leading publisher of business, motivation, and self-help authors. Do you have a manuscript or book idea that you would like to have considered for publication? Please visit **www.amgbook.com** or call **1.866.775.1696**

SURVIVING
THE
PERFECT
STORM

TABLE OF CONTENTS

INTRODUCTION

Who Needs Retirement Planning?

Here's a sobering fact: Most people put more research into buying a new washer or planning a vacation than they do into planning for their retirement.

Let's be honest. In terms of mapping out our financial futures, most of us go through life on cruise control. We come out of high school thinking about the next step: college, a trade school, a job. Maybe we get married and start having kids. Our day-to-day lives take up all of our attention, and we spend the next ten years or so focused on creating careers and sorting out our relationships: Who does which chores, who pays the bills, grocery shops, picks up and drops off the kids, who handles which aspects of the partnership. Somewhere in the backs of our minds we occasionally think, *I need to get around to thinking about retirement, but that's something I can worry about later because right now I'm so focused on getting my career up and running and starting a family.*

When we're young, we're concentrating on how to improve our positions in life so that we can accumulate the things we want in order to be comfortable. We're thinking, *I want a truck or a flat-screen TV. I want to be able to send my kids to this school, or get that gift for my spouse.* We spend a lot of time trying to get from here to there. We're not looking ahead to sixty-five because it's so far away that it's hard to even imagine it.

The following is by way of background, so you understand a little about how and why the economy works the way it does: If you think about it, we, as consumers, drive the economy. How do we know this? When America was attacked on 9/11, one of the first things President Bush did was go on television and tell America to not let the terrorists win – go shopping. He even handed out money to everybody. Do you remember getting those $300 checks? Remember when the economy started to fall in June 2008? President Bush again came to the rescue with handouts. President Obama did it again in 2009 and 2010. They both understood that for our economy and our market to move forward, we need America to shop and consume.

With that in mind, the following is a little about the American consumer: A great amount of work goes into researching demographics. Federal and state governments use the information to allocate resources for, among other things, building new schools. Businesses use it to determine which items to stock for the holidays or to carry on the menu. Think about McDonald's and its "healthy menu." It is there because demographic studies suggest that if McDonald's wants to continue to be the largest fast-food restaurant in the world, it has to appeal to an aging population that is becoming more and more health conscious.

That research provides some interesting insights into how the typical person lives his or her life. For example, the average person gets married around the age of twenty-six and has kids between the ages of twenty-eight and thirty. We purchase our first home by age thirty, and we spend more money on potato chips at age forty-four than we do at any other point in our lives. We know when people consume the most wine, use dry cleaners, and go camping. Basically, the government can measure almost every aspect of our lives.

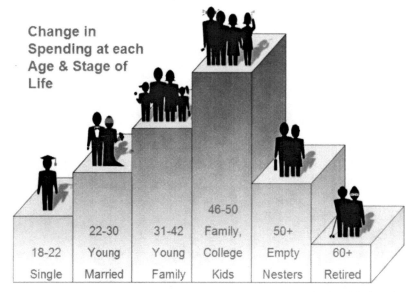

Copyright HS Dent 2009

Think about when we had children. We put all our energy into figuring out how to raise them right and how to provide for them and give them the things that are important along with how we're going to pay for it all. Before you know it, the kids are teenagers, and there's college to consider. At this point, as parents, our careers are blossoming. We're starting to grow into our jobs and take on more responsibility at work, but now there's more responsibility at home and, again, it's all about raising a family and taking care of our spouses. Next thing we know, we have kids going off to college. We're fifty, fifty-two, fifty-three years old, and what occurs to us is *Oh, my gosh, I want to retire in ten years, but do I have enough money?*

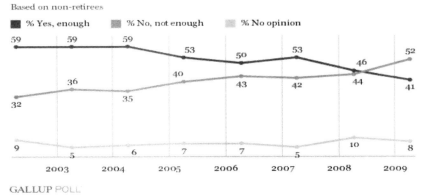

When you retire, do you think you will have enough money to live comfortably, or not?

Based on non-retirees

■ % Yes, enough   ■ % No, not enough   ■ % No opinion

GALLUP POLL

We've been so busy taking care of all these other demands that putting off planning seems like the natural course of things. That's what our parents did. That's what our grandparents did. That's what we see our friends and neighbors do. We all put off things that we can do later and focus on the challenges in front of us today.

Think about how we deal with our health, or even just repairs and maintenance on the house. Everybody always says, "Look, that's

14

something that can wait a couple of weeks," or "That's something we can do next year." People treat their retirement the same way. It's something we can wait for, something we'll take care of next week or next month or next year. Unfortunately, "next year" comes when people are fifty or fifty-five years old. That's when it hits us that we have so little time, and we get a little panicky. Even though we make more money between the ages of fifty and sixty than at any other point in our lives, it's almost a panic mode when we realize that – wow! – we have to start stashing away tons and tons of money just to get where we need to be, to maintain the vision of what retirement looks like. (That is actually an interesting question we'll discuss later: What does retirement look like? Have you thought about what you are doing on Tuesday? What did you do this week, this month? Is your spouse on the same page? More about this important thought later.)

At that point, if you're like most people, you start asking yourself, how little can I actually live on? I've worked hard all my life, and I'm going to get to retirement and have to scrimp and save and live meagerly so I don't have to work anymore. But that's not a way to go through retirement. That's not a way to live, worried about covering your bills or whether you can afford a steak dinner because you didn't save. Your income was $100,000 a year, and now you're going to retire on $40,000? That's just poor planning across the board.

The bottom line is that if you want to have the retirement you've dreamed of, that you envisioned when you were twenty, and twenty-five, and thirty years old, you should have started saving when you were twenty, twenty-five, and thirty years old. If the goal is to have $30,000 or $40,000 a year from your retirement fund, and you assume a 5 percent yield from your investments (and I am not sure that you can assume a 5 percent yield), you've got to have $1 million saved – and this doesn't even factor in inflation.

FOR BEST RESULTS, START SAVING EARLY!

If you start saving for $1 million when you're twenty-one or twenty-two years old, you'll have to put away $186 a month. If you wait until you're thirty-five years old – and this goes to time-valued money – then all of a sudden you'll have to put away $418 a month. If you wait until you're fifty, you'll have to put away $1,475 a month.

You can see how it's easier to achieve success if you are disciplined and start early, which goes back to what I've been talking about: planning. We tell our kids to do their homework ahead of time. We tell our kids to plan for college. We tell our kids to prepare, to get things done today because they don't know what's going to happen tomorrow. We teach our kids to take care of things now and not to procrastinate, and yet we're victims of our own procrastination. We fail to have the retirement we envision because we don't do what we're trying to teach our kids to do, which is to plan for tomorrow.

Why don't we practice what we preach? I think it's because somehow that particular aspect of our life is too far away and seems too scary, or too difficult to face, and nobody understands the rules: How much? When? How? Where will I live? Will I have enough? What about my kids? But I also think that the problem is that we're so preoccupied by the immediacy of life that it becomes one of those things that we think can wait. When you get that little mole on your forearm or your back, you say, "I'll go to the doctor next week." Then you get sidetracked and fifteen things happen, so you never get it done. It's one thing after another after another, and suddenly here you are three years later, and it turns out you have a cancerous growth that has spread. Had you gone to see the doctor immediately, he would have taken care of it, but it was one of those things that didn't seem to demand your immediate attention amid the distractions of everyday life, so you weren't thinking about it.

That's the same thing that happens with our retirement. "Later" comes, and it's a disaster because we haven't planned all along. We can't, as a society, seem to think clearly about "later." If you think about how we feel about the stock market and how we feel about investments in general, it's all about the immediacy. Companies are the way they are nowadays because everybody wants instant gratification. They want that great return right this second, and they don't want to have to wait for it.

All of us complain that our kids are the same way. They want their rewards today instead of waiting and earning them. Instead of thinking about and looking at the future, they are busy focusing on the immediacy of now. Instead of thinking about the big picture and having a long-term plan for success, we think about the immediate:

Can we trust the kid with the good car? Do we have enough milk for the weekend? Did we pick up the dry cleaning?

If you take it to the next level and make a comparison to successful businesses, leaders of successful businesses don't just sit down on the first of January and say, "Okay, where do we want to be at the end of the year?" They have plans set for the next ten to twenty years out. The plans are on paper so they can be modified and massaged as circumstances change, but there's a real plan in place. If you hit the lottery, you don't have to save as much. But that doesn't mean that you don't save until you do hit the lottery, right?

PLAYING THE LOTTERY IS NOT
A RETIREMENT STRATEGY!

If you think about it, that probably describes the retirement planning of a third of the people out there. They're either going to hit the lottery or they're going to retire on Social Security. But you know what? Social Security retirement stinks.

The typical clients who come to me are between ages fifty-five and seventy. They're coming in because they're retiring in the next couple of years, or it could even be that they're retiring early. But what's scaring them is wondering whether or not they actually have enough money to do it. Given the volatility of the market, they are worried that they might run out of money, and having to go back to work at age seventy-five or eighty isn't a good plan for any of us. All of a sudden it's, "Okay, time's up. I can retire. What do I do?" This book is written for that person who is between fifty and seventy years of age and within ten years of retirement and who has not done the retirement planning that he or she was supposed to have done. It is also beneficial to that person who has already retired but is using the I-hope approach to surviving his or her retirement years.

My clients share the following traits:

1. They understand that taking unnecessary risk at this point of their lives doesn't make sense. It takes too long to recoup losses.

2. They want a safe, secure, reliable, and predictable income plan, one they and their spouse or significant other will not run out of.

3. They want a financial plan that is verifiable, understandable, and based on real numbers, not assumptions and hypotheticals.

If this sounds like you, this book is for you.

Here's an uncomfortable truth, one you've probably noticed by now: Even the best-made plans can unravel, especially if you don't – or can't – follow common sense and recommendations.

A lady named Nancy came to me in 2000. She had worked for a big corporation, and like most long-term employees she was loyal to her company, to a fault. She had about $300,000 when she retired plus her Social Security, and all of that nest egg was in company stock. We discussed diversifying her portfolio and getting some of that money out of her company stock, but she didn't want to sell the stock because the company had always been so good to her and the stock had done well over time. Nancy felt that since her company had always taken care of her, selling the stock would be disloyal. But she did have an income requirement. She was taking about $2,500 a month from her stock

Well, $2,500 from her stock in the late '90s was fine because her company was zooming along. The problem became that in 2000, when the market dropped about 25 percent across the board, her company's stock dropped even further. Over the course of three years, her company's stock went from almost $332 a share to about $227 a share, and finally settled down to about $26 a share as of the writing of this book. Even though we told her all along, "You are going to run out of money. You can't keep doing this," she kept spending at the same rate because that was her lifestyle and because she was so sure that the company would take care of her.

Over time, the account dwindled down to about $20,000. She continued spending at the same rate, doing repairs and maintenance on her house, and fixing things up. She still wanted to travel and she was very socially active with the Red Hat society. In the end, she was forced to change her lifestyle, to stop spending and enjoying the retirement she'd envisioned because she no longer had the resources. We finally resorted to a reverse mortgage on her house and took cash out so she could have that extra money that she was looking for – the money she needed to take care of the repairs and maintenance on the house. We are not talking about travel and enjoying retirement but strictly looking at her ability to maintain her home.

That money wasn't invested in the stock market. She put it in a bank account for safekeeping and used it properly, but she ended up spending it over the course of several years. By 2006 she was running short again. She was very fortunate. Because the housing market was still zooming, her house actually went up in value and she was able to do another reverse mortgage. She did a second one and pulled out an extra $80,000 from her house.

Now, there are a couple of things to remember here: Every time she did a reverse mortgage, the transaction cost for her was about $15,000. She gave up $30,000 in fees so that she could try to maintain her style of living because she hadn't planned properly. She had never saved adequately for retirement, based on her spending needs, and more important, she had all her eggs in one basket. She had a year-and-a-half's worth of money, but since 2008 she's been living on her monthly $1,194 Social Security check. And because she has a child with special needs, she's relying on her sister and nieces and nephews to help her out. She's in that position for reasons I'll explain further on, having to do with what is called "the sequence of returns." We'll discuss this later as we're talking about how to allocate properly and how much risk you should be taking, but the simplest explanation for Nancy's problems is that she didn't plan properly. She didn't think about how much money she was going to need. She was taking out too much money all along, and she didn't consider how long she'd need that money to last.

Nancy's a prime example of what happens when people aren't thinking about what happens down the road. Unfortunately, she's not unique. Here's another story, with a slightly happier ending. Adam and his wife came to us back in 2000, and we designed a plan for them based on an income of $60,000 a year. We knew the markets would go up and down, and we planned a pretty conservative portfolio. When Adam retired, he was fifty-seven. Their goal was to take $60,000 a year and adjust it for inflation until Adam was sixty-six, which was his full retirement age for Social Security purposes.

Well, as often happens, things changed a little bit. At the beginning, Adam and his wife were feeling pretty good because our allocation for them in the market was doing well. They started spending more. When we talked about what changes they were going to make in the next couple of years, they said that they wanted to take out an extra $1,500 a month from the accounts because they wanted to buy a timeshare for the family at a resort so that they could vacation together.

Then they put an addition onto the house, so they took another mortgage out on their house because they needed an extra $500 a month. Instead of living on $60,000 as planned, suddenly they needed $84,000. The plan did not account for $84,000, rather, it accounted for $60,000. They'd come to us with an I-think approach and we put a plan in place that would have maintained their income up to age ninety-five. If they ran out of money at age ninety-five, at that point they would do a reverse mortgage on their house. But even at that point they were thinking their house would continue to appreciate at the rate of 5 to 10 percent per year. We explained to them that, at best, we were willing to use 50 percent of the current value of the house as a fallback position down the road because houses go up and down in value, and it seemed to me that houses were going up too fast and that couldn't last forever. I'm not going to tell you I saw a 50 percent crash coming in the housing market because I didn't, but nevertheless, we weren't willing to be as aggressive with the projections as they wanted us to be.

Fast forward to 2007 and they're taking $84,000 a year out. Adam turns sixty-six years of age and it's time for him and his wife, Sarah, to start taking Social Security. The goal had always been that when they started taking Social Security, we'd reduce the withdrawal from their investment accounts by the same amount. Between the two of them they were going to get almost $35,000 a year in Social Security, which meant we could decrease withdrawals by almost $35,000.

But instead of following the more prudent course, they chose to continue taking the $35,000 withdrawals because they saw their accounts growing. We'd had many conversations about the folly of relying on the market to go up consistently because there are good years and bad years. In 2008 they lost 10 percent. They only lost 10 percent even though the market lost 40 percent because we were proactive in how we were managing the accounts. Keep in mind that we only lost 10 percent on the money that was "extra." Remember that I have said that our plan always has a safe, steady, reliable, and predictable income stream, so that portion of their portfolio was fine, but it wasn't designed to create an extra $35,000 a year, and that was what caused the problem.

Taking the money out of the market in 2008 was fine because we had already done that. The problem was that when we wanted to go back in, they were so shell-shocked from their previous losses that they didn't want to get back in. That meant that they missed almost all of 2009's rally. Meanwhile, they were still taking out more than $70,000 a year because they needed not only the $60,000 they were living on, but also $24,000 to pay for the addition to their house and the timeshare. That $84,000 was after taxes, so it came to about $70,000 in pretax dollars from their investments plus the $35,000 they were receiving from Social Security.

People make the mistake of assuming that they're going to be able to live comfortably on less in retirement because their expenses will go down, but they don't. In the case of Adam and Sarah, we had created a plan based on their income needs. Those needs changed when they purchased a time-share and put an addition onto their home. The results were Adam had to go back to work to make sure that they would not run out of money. He worked at a home improvement store, making about $30,000 a year so they could afford to pay for the condo and the addition to their house. So where is the slightly happier ending? Adam loves his job and feels as if he is being productive again. He still has the time he wants and needs for his children and grandchildren and, most important, he sees the light at the end of the tunnel. Fortunately, we were able to convince him to take only ten-year mortgages, so by the time he turns seventy-five years of age, he will be able to live comfortably on his Social Security and his investments.

One key planning factor that is often ignored is that most of us in the first eight or ten years of retirement spend substantially more than we had envisioned because of the proverbial round-to-it list, aka the honey-do list. All of a sudden we find ourselves with time and energy, and we're traveling to places we always wanted to travel but couldn't because we were raising kids and working. We're doing projects. We're getting involved in the community, and thinking, "Gee, how did I get anything done having to work all day because I'm busy all day long?"

Statistically what we see is that an average person retires at age sixty-two. From sixty-two to seventy years of age, your spending actually increases every year because you're doing more things, enjoying your new freedom. Sometime around seventy to seventy-two years of age, you plateau and drop off a little bit, and by seventy-five years of age you see a pretty significant dip in spending, mostly because at around seventy-five years of age, naptime looks pretty good. You're slowing down physically, and it's not that you don't still want to do things, but now you are doing them at a more leisurely pace. It's not a frantic, active 24/7 lifestyle. You're not out playing tennis every day. In those early years people spend more, and you need to plan for that, but when things start slowing down, you need less money, and that should be part of your overall retirement plan also. People always think, "How much am I going to need?" not "How do I get there? Is it going to be enough? How do I take it out?" Those questions too should all be part of the planning process.

About me

I grew up in one of those epically dysfunctional families like something out of the proverbial movie of the week. I was in and out of foster homes. We lived hand-to-mouth. We were one of those families that were sponsored for Christmas. I remember a local church took us on summer vacations. Through divorces and all kinds of chaos, I've watched my parents and my adopted parents struggle to make ends meet not only when we were growing up but also as they got into retirement.

My adopted mother and her husband live on meager Social Security in West Virginia – four hours away from their thirteen grandkids – because that's where they could afford to live. My birth mother lives in a little town in Northern California. She's on disability, so she still gets housing, but my sister and I help supplement her because she lives strictly on disability income. I've seen this style of living up very close and personal. It's a style in which people can't afford to buy clothes and have to weigh whether or not they can have lunch at the deli this month or even afford to keep a pet.

Seeing this as I grew up left a lasting impression. I didn't want to be in that position. I wanted to tell people and show people that this is the reality for a significant portion of America. The average American retires with less than $50,000 of assets beyond his/her home and only Social Security as his/her income. That is no way to go through retirement. You've worked hard all your life, and you're coming up to what are supposed to be your golden years when you sit back and enjoy the fruits of your labor – and there's no fruit. It's a barren tree. As you can tell, for me, this is an issue with a lot of personal resonance.

I did my undergraduate work at the University of Baltimore and attended graduate school at American University before transferring and completing law school at the Catholic University of America. On the law side, my background was estate planning. I worked for an estate-planning firm when I came out of law school, and I went on to get my master's degree in taxation. (Attorneys do it a little bit backward. We get our doctoral degree first, which is the actual law degree, the Juris Doctor (JD). We get a master's degree second, which is a higher degree for attorneys.) I have a master's degree in taxation because, as disturbing as it sounds, I truly enjoy the tax field. In my profession it's one of the last areas of sheer creativity that you can really manipulate and play with. The rules are so black and white with almost everything, but in the tax field you actually have an opportunity to work in the gray areas. Taxation never says, "This is what you can do." It's about what you can't do. You can be very creative tax-wise, not just with income tax, but also with estate planning, which contains a lot of wiggle room in which to make things work to the advantage of your clients.

I'm also a financial planner. I'm asked sometimes what the difference is between a financial planner and a financial advisor, stockbroker, investment advisor, or an insurance agent. It's an important distinction. A financial planner has a fiduciary duty to put the interests of the client first. From my perspective, all the rest are just salesmen whose only obligation is to make sure whatever investment recommendation they make is suitable at the moment. The work of a financial advisor is more about the moment, about the individual transaction that's about to occur. In contrast, a financial planner looks at the big financial picture and helps you fine-tune each aspect of it. A financial advisor is going to talk to you about an investment. A financial planner is going to design a plan that incorporates not only the investment but how much risk you should be taking (notice we don't ask about how much risk you should tolerate, but rather, how much do you *have* to tolerate), and how you're going to distribute the investment tax-efficiently to you and to your spouse and to your heirs.

As financial planners, we talk to you about estate planning and about tax planning. That includes risk mitigation, which is everything from checking that you've got enough homeowner's and auto insurance to making sure that you're not overpaying for it. We look at long-term care, either in-home or otherwise, and how it will be paid for. We examine legacy issues and how to pass on your hard-earned assets to the next generation as tax-efficiently as possible as well as probate free. If there's a dollar sign involved in it, a financial planner will have some sort of input and impact with regard to how you're going to use that dollar.

Maybe you're reading this and saying to yourself, "I'm fifty years old. It's too late, right?" The answer is that it's *never too late to create the plan.* The longer you wait, the fewer options you have, but it's never too late to create the plan, even if you're sixty years old and you're getting ready to retire, or even if you're seventy and already retired. We are all living longer, and having a plan to ensure you are living the retirement you envisioned is always important because it will bring peace of mind, not only to you, but also to your spouse, family, and loved ones. If they know that you have a plan and have clearly thought out your future, they too can rest assured and sleep better at night.

Let's talk a little about where you put your retirement money. There is no crystal ball to tell me what's going happen in the stock market, but I do know a couple of things about the stock market that always are correct. Here they are: The stock market will go up, and the stock market will go down. For people who want to take stress out of their lives about the uncertainty of the stock market, who want a plan to create a predictable, reliable, secure income stream, there are ways to do it so that you're basically creating your own pension. You won't have to care whether the stock market goes up or down because it won't impact your day-to-day life. It won't impact your ability to go buy a cup of coffee, to have lunch, to make a car payment, to pay for your insurance, to take care of your dogs, or to take the grandkids on a cruise. It doesn't impact those things because the plan you have in place has you covered regardless of market gyrations.

I see my job as your planner as analogous to that stereotypical Boy Scout, holding the groceries and helping the little old lady across the road. A financial planner is supposed to do the same thing for you in guiding your steps and helping you out. When the stock market's doing really well and you're really excited about how everything's going, my job is to hold your hand to keep you from running into traffic. Conversely, when the stock market's going crazy and being stupid and you're scared to death, my job is to hold your hand and walk you through the traffic to make sure we're not getting run over.

It's about mitigating uncertainty so that you can sleep at night. It's adventurous and romantic to be struggling when you're young. It's not so much fun when you're moving into your retirement years. The secret is to have a plan on paper, a plan that is of course subject to adjustments and tweaking as circumstances change, but a real plan, crafted in agreement with your spouse.

Once you have that plan, the next question to ask yourself is, how am I going to make my plan come true? That's where I come in and what this book is meant to help you figure out.

CHAPTER ONE

THE MAKING OF
A PERFECT STORM

This is not one of those personal finance books that resorts to scare tactics or fear-mongering to try to panic you by going on about all the horrible things that are going to happen. With that said, and no matter which political party wins the next election, the next seven to ten years are going be a long, hard slog. We're on the verge of a perfect financial storm, and it's worth taking a few moments to consider how we came to find ourselves here.

In 1946 men came home from World War II. They settled down and started making babies, a lot of babies. Between '46 and the Korean War, a population chart would show an almost straight-up line of baby-making: the Baby Boom. There's a little dip at the start of the Korean War because when men go off to war they stop making babies, but a couple of years later, they're home and they're back to making babies again. Between '46 and '62, a lot of babies were made, and I mean a *lot* of them.

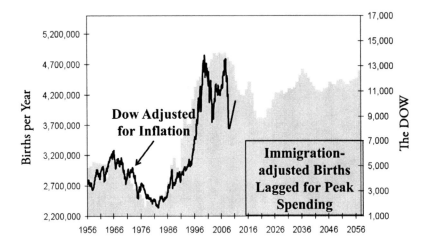

All those babies ultimately grew up and became consumers, and here's what we know about that: Consumers have what are called *predictable spending habits*. The government does a consumer expenditure survey every year, in which it studies 60,000 American families. These 60,000 American families report what they spend their money on, kind of like the Nielsen ratings do for TV and radio. Some interesting patterns come out when you look at these consumer expenditure survey results. Statistically speaking, a majority of us go off to college or some sort of trade school at age eighteen or nineteen. We spend three to five years getting trained in some particular field of work. When we're done training, we go get a job in that particular industry.

As we all know, any time you hire somebody new, he's initially more of a burden than a benefit because it takes him several years to become truly productive in what he's doing. That means by the time he's twenty-five or twenty-six years old, he's a productive member of the company, producing more benefit or more revenue or more widgets for the company than it costs the company to have him in place.

You get to be twenty-five or twenty-six years old and you start thinking about settling down. Typically, we get married between the ages of twenty-six and twenty-eight. When we first get married, we live in apartments and condos. Most of us don't go out and buy a house. We have our first child between the ages of twenty-eight and thirty. At that point we look for our first house, and it's typically a smaller house because our income is less. Now we're spending a little more of our income because we are spending more money on our children. We want them to have all those things that we didn't have, and we want them to have a better life that we did. This is especially true for the Baby Boomers, those who were born between '46 and '62. *Their* parents grew up in the Great Depression, so they had this very frugal I-can't-spend-it-because-I'm-so-afraid-I'm-going-to-lose-it mentality. The Baby Boomers pushed back against that, saying "We're going to spend. We're not going be like our parents, who were so ridiculously tight."

So we get to age thirty. We have a kid, and we've bought our first house. Sometime between thirty and thirty-five years of age we have our second kid. The average American family has 2.3 children (I know. That .3 is kind of scary, but we do have 2.3 children) and we buy a bigger house. By age fifty, we've bought the biggest house we're ever going to buy – and that's an important point that we'll come back to and discuss further along. Here's what happens between ages forty and fifty for most of us: We have teenagers in the house, and anybody who has ever raised teenagers knows what teenagers do.

They get up in the morning – actually, more like two in the afternoon – and they open their mouths and they start eating.

I have two boys. My kids will get up at two in the afternoon and they will have a bowl of cereal. Then they'll ask their mom to make some pancakes. Then they'll go play on the computer, and they'll come back around four thirty or five and have a sandwich and a bag of potato chips. Then they'll have dinner, and top that off with a bowl of ice cream, another bowl of cereal, some popcorn, a couple slices of pizza, another bag of chips and six sodas – and it's only ten thirty at night. Caloric intake for teenagers is huge. They're consuming more calories between the ages of twelve and eighteen than they do at any other point in their lives because their bodies are going nuts.

But the corresponding extrapolation from that is that we spend more and more money on food so that they can have that intake. The result is that between the ages of forty and fifty, we spend more money than we do at any other point in our lives. But it isn't just grocery shopping. It is clothes, activities, driving, technology (who doesn't have a child or grandchild with the latest smart phone growing out of her/his ear?). Again, going back to the consumer expenditure survey, we spend more money on potato chips at age forty-four than we do at any other point, and that's not because we're eating them. At age forty-four, we're thinking about salads and oatmeal and our bulging waistlines, but we're buying potato chips for our kids.

Potato Chip Purchases Vs. Age

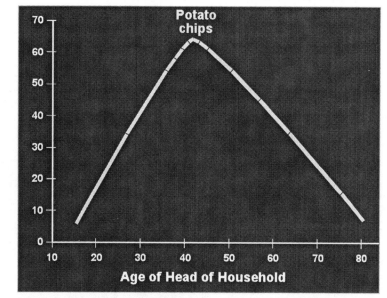

Source: Consumer Expenditure Survey

Consumer consumption is 70 percent of gross domestic product. That means that 70 percent of all production and all the spending that goes on in the United States is driven by our buying stuff. That's everything from computers for our teenagers to cars for our teenagers, to bicycles and clothes and whatever the latest toy is: the iPad, the iPhone, the iWhatever. We spend a boatload of money on raising kids.

Now let's go back and think about what we said happened on 9/11. Right after 9/11, President Bush went on national television, and one of the things that he stressed was that we couldn't let those terrorists win – go shopping. If you remember back to that, he sent you $300. In 2008, when the stock market was crashing, Bush sent you more money. From the crash of 2008 through the writing of this book, President Obama has been sending money left and right to middle America through rebates, energy credits, education credits, payroll tax cuts, Making America Work credits; anything and everything the administration could think of to get more money into our pockets, hoping that we would go out and spend it.

That's so important because the only way this economy is going to turn around again is for people to start buying stuff again. Employers are not going to hire more people just because they pay lower taxes, or because they have lower pension obligations. They can have trillions and trillions of dollars on their books, but they're not going to hire new workers until people start consuming. It doesn't matter how many widgets you can build or how cheaply. If people are not going to purchase them, you're not going to make them.

That's the crux of our economic problem right now: There's not enough consumption. The Chinese at one time had cooperatives making eight billion bicycles a month, but nobody was buying them. The fact that you can produce all this stuff and put all these people to work is completely irrelevant if nobody's buying it. That's where we are today, and that's where we're going to be for the near future – probably the next seven to ten years.

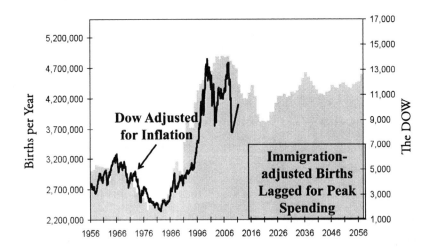

In this chart, we can see that as we overlay the Dow Jones Industrial Average, pushed forward for peak spending years, there seems to be a correlation between the rise in the Dow and when we, as consumers, spend money.

Why has this happened in this way? I mentioned before that around the ages of twenty-two to twenty-four you're gaining work experience because you've gone to college or you've gone to training school, and you've gotten your on-the-job training. By the time you're about twenty-five years old, you've started to become a productive member of the workforce, which means now you have some money to spend. So let's test our hypothesis: Take 1946, and add twenty-five years to that, bringing us to 1971.

In '71 the market was pathetic, but you saw the first Baby Boomers coming out of school and putting stress on employers. All of these people were entering the workforce and getting jobs, but they weren't being that productive because if you remember back to your own early experiences in employment, you spent your first year or two figuring out what the heck you were supposed to be doing. You might have been book smart, but you didn't actually know how to do anything. When I came out of law school I knew all sorts of law, but I didn't know how to fill out a form because I'd never had to do it. It took four to five years to figure out how to do things properly by learning from my more experienced coworkers. So at this point, the Boomers were twenty-two to twenty-five years old, and their learning curve was creating a drain on the economy.

Push forward five years to 1976-77. Things were still a little scary, but when these folks were thirty years old and just starting to have babies, we can see things were starting to get better. As more and more of these Boomers hit their early thirties and were having kids in the early '80s, the economy started to pick up. We had a larger and larger Baby Boomer generation becoming productive members of their workplaces, having babies, and spending money.

They were buying houses because they wanted nicer homes for their kids. By the early '80s we had a national savings rate of about 12 percent, but that savings rate would decline over the next twenty years as more and more Baby Boomers moved into this spending phase. They were accumulating more assets, but they were assets such as houses and refrigerators and cars, most of which are what we call depreciable assets, which lose value over time. You consume them, use them up, and then replace them.

Flash forward almost twenty years. By 2000 our savings rate was zero. We had been saving 12 percent, and within twenty years we were saving zero. That meant people in general were spending that much more money, first, because they were making more (fellow Boomers, we're the last generation that will make more money than our parents). It makes sense that the kids who were born in the '50s and '60s made more money than those born in the '30s and '40s, who in turn made more money than those born in the '10s and the '20s. Second, we were spending more because we were saving less.

While we as consumers were busy spending all this newfound money, the federal government spent it just as we did, expanding social welfare programs. By 2005 we had gone from a zero savings rate in 2000 to a savings rate of negative 5 to 8 percent, depending on what economist you ask. That means we were borrowing more money than we were making, and we're throwing that debt into the economy, which has huge, multiple ramifications on economic growth.

Let's look at the impact of purchasing a house. If you want to buy a house in Baltimore, Maryland, you're going to pay roughly $500,000 for a three-bedroom, two-bath house on a quarter-acre of land. If you buy a home from somebody who's been living in that house for ten years, the economic impact is zero because all we're really doing is transferring an existing asset for cash from one person to another. That has no economic benefit, or almost no economic benefit. The lawyers get paid, and the real estate agents get paid, and there's some clerk someplace shuffling paperwork, but the economic benefits are nominal. Between 5 and 10 percent of the purchase value is paid out to somebody else in salaries and wages, but everything else is just transferred between two people.

Compare that to the economic impact of buying a house in a brand-new development. Here's where you can see the significant impact that resulted from the Baby Boomers coming of age economically. They wanted more houses and bigger houses, so builders went on a construction spree.

Let's say John Builder goes out and acquires a hundred acres of land. It's very unlikely that he can pay cash for it, so he borrows $1 million to buy that land, and he's paying that bank back at the rate of $5,000 a month. Now, he has to go out and hire a design team to plot out the development so that he can put his 200 homes on this land. He's paying people who in turn hire the surveyors. Then he has to hire somebody else to clear the land. Remember, he paid $1 million for the land and now he needs revenue to pay the people who are doing the surveys and the people who are doing the clearing, so he borrows another $1 million to fund all this. Now he's paying one bank $5,000 a month and paying another bank $5,000 a month, but he has $2 million, half to put into this property and the other half to spend on developing this property. He's hired people who not only hire others but have to purchase equipment to clear the land. Somebody had to make the equipment for them to buy, and the ripple effect keeps moving down the road. In addition, once the land is cleared, the developer has to hire somebody else to put in the infrastructure: sewer pipes, roads, curbs, and sidewalks. Then he has to build each of the houses, putting to work those people who cut timber, ship timber, and ship drywall. The people who move those materials – on the trucking side, the loading side, the docks if it's being shipped via water, the railroads if it's going that way – all of these people make a little bit of money too.

John the Builder puts up his model home and sells it. That buyer gets a $500,000 loan from the bank, which makes money on that loan, and gives John the Builder $500,000, with which he builds another house.

Can you see the impact of purchasing a new home in comparison with buying an existing one? The problem we have just from that perspective is that most Baby Boomers are now all fifty years of age or older. And you know what? We're all done buying the biggest home we're ever going to own. We're all done moving upward.

If you refer back to the birth chart that we've shown you, you'll see from '62 to '75 the birth rate dropped precipitously.

Immigration Adjusted Birth Index

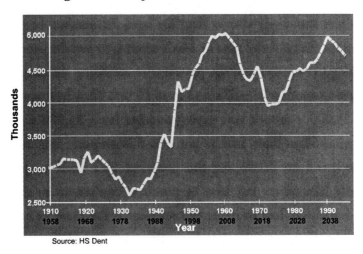

Source: HS Dent

It was a period of less and less consumption because there were fewer and fewer people to do the consuming. We've all heard about how wonderful China is going to be economically, and we've seen it do really well over the last ten years. We've all heard how wonderful India is going to be, and it's been doing extremely well over the last ten years. Is it because of their economic systems? Is it because of their governments? Is it because they have raw materials? Is it because they have land?

No, it's because those are the number-one and number-two largest populations in the world with huge populations between the ages of thirty and fifty, and thirty- to fifty-year-olds even in developing countries spend as much money as they're ever going to spend on raising their kids.

Let's look at Japan and make the comparison to the Japanese economy and birthrates. Think back to the early years of Ronald Reagan's presidency. Reagan was the champion for capitalism and the free-market society: Let business run and it will take care of everything and the economy will prosper. But one thing he did was somewhat counterintuitive to his stated ideology. In the early '80s, Japan was becoming an economic superpower. Japanese investors bought Rockefeller Center. They bought half of California, and if you have ever had the pleasure of living in or vacationing in Hawaii, I am pretty sure they actually own the state. As Americans, we were afraid that the Japanese, who didn't defeat us militarily, were going to take us over economically. They were an economic juggernaut. Ronald Reagan, the champion of capitalism, started throwing up tariffs to protect our economy from those mean ol' Japanese, and a huge trade war ensued.

Let's look at what happened to Japan in the '80s and '90s. Its stock market zoomed from '83-'84 to '90. Ours paled in comparison.

Japanese Nikkei Index
Jan 1984 – Jan 1990

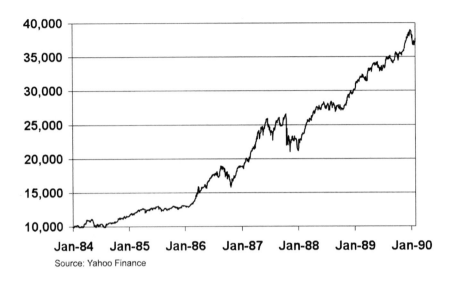

Source: Yahoo Finance

Let's look at their birthrates. Japanese men came home from the war in 1945 and they made babies just like American men did until about 1950.

Japan Birth Index
47-Year Birth Lag

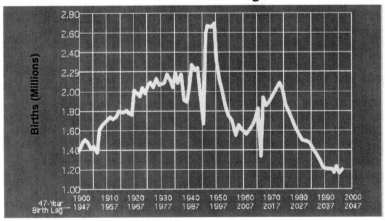

Source: Japan Ministry of Internal Affairs and Communication

In 1950 Japanese businessmen came over to the United States and said, "We really want to be an economic superpower as you guys are." They looked at our manufacturing plants, took our plans back to Japan, tried it our way for a couple of years, and decided it was really not working very well. The quality wasn't there. They made some modifications following their philosophical beliefs on how to do things, and then they kicked our butts in manufacturing for the next thirty or forty years and their economy zoomed. The important take-away here is that in 1950 they slowed down on making babies and focused on expanding their economy. The population growth was a straight-up line and then a straight-down line. Their markets zoomed from about '82-'83 up to about '91 and then what happened in '91? The Nikkei, the Japanese version of the Dow, had reached almost 40,000. Within five years it was down to 5,000. Over the last twenty years it's hovered in the 5,000 to 10,000 range and can't get out of its own way.

Japanese Stock Market vs. Change in Japanese Consumer Spending 1987 – 2005

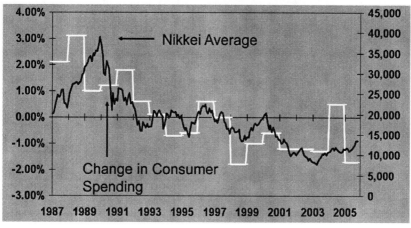

Source: Japanese Family Income and Expenditure Survey

Here's what Japan did from the '90s to 2011 trying to stimulate its economy: It offered interest rates of 0 percent for almost a decade. Hmm, sounds eerily familiar, doesn't it? It offered stimulus payments to the people – "Go spend money." Again, this sounds very familiar. When Japanese corporations started failing and going under, when the banks started failing and going under, Japan took the too-big-to-fail approach and didn't let them fail.

Now, our economy is much larger, and our population is much more diverse. I don't think we're in as bad a shape as Japan was, but certainly until December of 2010, Japan was the world's second-largest economy. Now it's the world's third-largest economy.

Is it fair to say that if it could happen to the world's second largest economy, it could happen to the world's largest? It's fair to say that we're following in the footsteps of Japan. It's not a perfect analogy because our population is much larger, our economy is much larger, and the diversification is much broader. But the problem is that we're looking a lot like Japan in what we're doing to hold our economy together, and it's fair to assume that it's not going to be different for us than it was for Japan.

Why would we expect it to be any different? Think about this: The Japanese lost 40 percent of their land value. Housing prices dropped 40 percent. In the United States there's always plenty of room to grow if that's what you want to do. But Japan is an island, so you can't build up any more, and housing prices *still* dropped. When the largest percentage of our population that has purchasing power has gone beyond age fifty, why would we think that anybody's going to be there to buy our homes? Why is the collapse of the housing market a surprise at all? It shouldn't be. We've been warned for decades that that there would not be enough children to grow up and pay into the Social Security system to support the Baby Boomers as they aged. If we knew that was the case, why did we think there would be enough people to buy our houses? That's the disconnect we have.

What happens demographically from age fifty to age sixty-two is that we save. We pay down debt, which is good for us but horrible for the economy because it's not putting new money into the economy. We save for our retirement, which is good for us individually, but, again, bad for the economy because we're not spending it. We're putting it into the stock markets, banks, or even under the mattress. I don't care how many shares of stock you buy. If that company is not selling widgets, it's not hiring people, and the economy is not going to expand. That doesn't mean the company can't be profitable because it can trim and trim and cut the fat. Still, only big, solid companies with cash reserves will survive this contraction.

And also keep in mind that the Baby Boomers just started turning sixty-two years of age a couple of years ago, and in 2011 they started getting Medicare. The economy was already in trouble in 2008 when they started receiving Social Security. Now the Boomers are going on Medicare, and we're only at the front end of the wave. Just wait another ten years, when all the Baby Boomers want Medicare.

Now, about the bright light I see at the end of it: Why do I think that we'll see a recovery in seven to ten years? There are some other factors at play that are beyond the scope of this conversation, but there are predictable, chartable cycles of the economy that seem to share some common patterns. They're not exact, but we seem to be in what's called a seventeen-year pattern. If you go back to '82, the market started zooming, and continued up to 1999, a great seventeen-year period. When did the market start tanking? If you look at about '63 or '64 to '81, the market was kind of flat and sideways. We had some real dips, including '71 and '72.

100 Years of the Dow

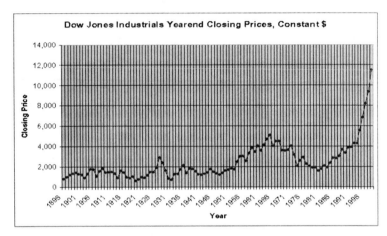

SOURCE: The Dow Jones Industrial Average is unmanaged and not available for direct investment. The payment of dividends is not reflected in the index return. Past Performance does not guarantee future results. SOURCE: classroomtools.com

1929-1946

17 Years of Down and Flat Market

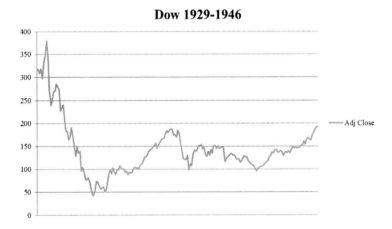

SOURCE: The Dow Jones Industrial Average is unmanaged and not available for direct investment. The payment of dividends is not reflected in the index return. Past Performance does not guarantee future results. SOURCE: classroomtools.com

DOW 1947-1964

17 Years of the Market Trending Upwards

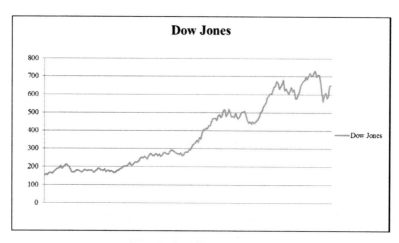

SOURCE: The Dow Jones Industrial Average is unmanaged and not available for direct investment. The payment of dividends is not reflected in the index return. Past Performance does not guarantee future results. SOURCE: yahoo.com

The 60's & 70's

17 More Years of Flat and Sideways Market

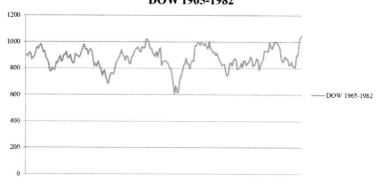

SOURCE: The Dow Jones Industrial Average is unmanaged and not available for direct investment. The payment of dividends is not reflected in the index return. Past Performance does not guarantee future results. SOURCE: yahoo.com

The 80's & 90's

17 Years of the Market Trending Upwards
DOW 1982-1999

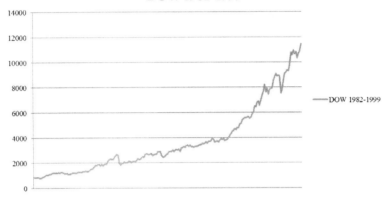

SOURCE: The Dow Jones Industrial Average is unmanaged and not available for direct investment. The payment of dividends is not reflected in the index return. Past Performance does not guarantee future results. SOURCE: yahoo.com

Dow 2000 until Present

What Do You Think?

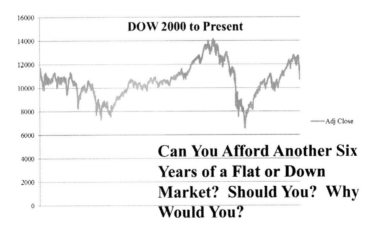

Can You Afford Another Six Years of a Flat or Down Market? Should You? Why Would You?

SOURCE: The Dow Jones Industrial Average is unmanaged and not available for direct investment. The payment of dividends is not reflected in the index return. Past Performance does not guarantee future results. SOURCE: yahoo.com August 11, 2011

In '29 to '46 the markets were horrible. Investors broke even. But from '47 to '62-'63, the markets did pretty well, as the charts show. There seem to be consistent seventeen-year patterns. There's no consistency in whether they're up or down or sideways, but they run in patterns. From '29 to '46 it was a down and sideways market. From '47 to basically '64 it was pretty much up. From '64 to '81 it was down and sideways, and from '82 to '99 it was up. From 2000 to at least today, most Americans who just bought and held stocks in the S&P and the Dow have lost money. I think if you look at it from a demographic point of view, a consumer-spending point of view, we probably have seven to ten years of this because the next boom will be created by those kids born '75 to '91.

Just as we did, as they get into that age range from thirty to fifty, they'll see the economy come back. We'll see them start to come into it in 2020, not in full force but enough to begin to drive the economy toward expansion again. Is there certainty with this? Of course not, but it does seem to fit a consistent pattern we have seen over the years. And, more important, this is why you need to plan.

If the government tampers with Social Security and Medicare in a dramatic way for the immediate population, it will have a devastating impact on them. Clearly the way in which Social Security and Medicare work is going to have to be modified, sooner or later, for those people who will be receiving it twenty to thirty years from now. In the meantime, there are all these people who have spent their working lives contributing to a program that they always assumed was going to be there to take care of them. When Social Security came into being, it wasn't designed for the masses. It was really designed for the working poor. It was meant to be a safety net for the most vulnerable: the elderly poor. Another point to remember is that since Social Security was created, our average life expectancy has increased significantly. Most people in the '30s died between the ages of fifty-five and sixty-five. Social Security was designed to be paid out to a small group of people for a relatively short period of time, maybe three to five years. Now people take Social Security at age sixty-two and live an additional thirty years. Coupled with the obligations created by Medicare, the system, as it stands, is unsustainable.

I think that in a civilized society it's a reasonable expectation that everyone should have access to health care, but the problem with Medicare is that it's designed to give everybody everything. Is there a solution? Perhaps, but it won't be easy, and implementing it will take significant courage on the part of our elected officials, something I don't have much confidence in.

We've talked about the predictable slowdown in consumer spending, combined with the increased demands on social programs, specifically between Social Security and Medicare, and the fact that the money isn't there to fund them.

Added to this is the death of the pension system as we know it. One of the reasons General Motors (GM) was willing to give basically all its stock to the United Auto Workers in 2008 was that the union took on all the pension and health care obligations for all retired employees. If GM couldn't find a way to keep those escalating costs funded, why did the union think it was better suited for the task?

And not only is the pension system failing from that perspective, it's failing us as individuals because businesses will find ways to restructure the pension systems they have in place. People think their employers can't change the terms of their pension plans after the fact, but there are plenty of court cases across America in which those pension systems get renegotiated. We've seen companies bankrupt their pension systems and retirees get fifty cents on the dollar. We call that "moving to a new neighborhood." One, your pension gets cut in half while you're living, and two, your surviving spouse gets even less money because of the election you made regarding survivor benefits. The third part of the pension problem is that the notion of being able to depend on a pension in retirement led people away from saving for themselves. You knew you had a pension, so you didn't have to worry about saving money. You could spend what you wanted to spend because you had that cushion to fall back on. When that cushion is suddenly pulled away, which is happening for a lot of people who didn't anticipate it, what can you do?

That's why you need to have a plan. It allows you to say, "I'd rather have too much and not need it than hope that I'm going to have it and not get it." If you plan ahead under the assumption that it's not going to be there for you, imagine how much nicer retirement's going to be if it turns out it's there after all? It's kind of like cleaning the house, lifting up the seat cushions, and finding $10. It's nice to have that extra money.

Don't go with a plan based on what you hope is going to happen or what you assume is going to happen. Stop assuming something's going to happen. Use simple math. One and one are always two. One plus "I think I might get an 8 percent return, but it could be a negative 8 percent, so I might be at a negative 7 percent instead" just doesn't cut it. It's up to you. You can take a nominal amount of risk and have predictable, dependable income during retirement, or you can take a boatload of risk. You might end up driving a Ferrari and living on a sailboat, or you could be renting a room and working at Walmart because the big "if" is there. You want certainty. There's nothing worse than uncertainty in our lives in general, and there's really nothing worse than uncertainty when you get to retirement. If you have a plan based on straight math and facts, you'll know what you need to have saved in order to retire comfortably.

You have a choice. You can take a rate of return that's based on assumptions, or you can take a rate of return that's fixed: "This is what I'm going to earn on it, and it doesn't change." Personally, I like "doesn't change." It might not be glamorous or sexy, but it's safe.

I always equate it to playing baseball. We have choices on how we play. Everybody likes to go watch the home-run hitters. They're always disappointed when they strike out, but they love it when they hit a home run. I much prefer that guy who always gets a walk and always gets on base. Once in a while he gets a double, but he always gets on base and he never strikes out. That's like an interest rate. The interest rate might be low, but you're always getting something. If you want certainty in your plan, if you want to know where you're going to be at a specified point in your life and whether you can afford to retire, the plan should say, "I'm going to invest X number of dollars per month at this rate of return, which will result in this much money at my retirement age, and from that retirement nest egg I will be able to withdraw this much money per year to meet my living needs" – my *needs*, not my *wants*. That's what people need to distinguish. I want to play golf every Friday, but if I can't, I still need to eat. I want to go skiing twice a year out in Tahoe, but if I can't, I still need to make my car insurance payment.

The intent of this book is to help you to make that safe, secure plan, the one that will insure your needs in retirement. Even if it's late in the game, you can take steps to create the income you need. Now, let's look at how we're going to create that plan.

MIKE'S BOTTOM LINE

Bumpy times are ahead for the economy, but you can still protect yourself and your retirement by smart planning.

CHAPTER TWO

CREATING THE PLAN

H ave you already had that conversation with your spouse, the one about how you see retirement? If you haven't, do it now. A good friend of mine, Doug Carter, introduced me to this exercise. I recommend that you each sit down separately from each other and write out your expectations of what your lives in retirement will be. What does this week look like? What did I do today? What does the month look like?

What does my future look like?

The goal of this worksheet is to set reasonable expectations of what retirement looks like to each of you. Too often we spend time dreaming about retirement but never discuss what that dream may look like. You will be spending a considerable amount of time together. You should be on the same page on what that time may look like.

I plan to retire at age_____

Quality of life – what does it look like?

_____

_____

_____

_____

What three activities would I like to do this week?

_____

_____

_____

_____

This month I intend to:

_____

_____

_____

_____

I want to improve the following:

_____

_____

_____

_____

Today my spouse and I did:

_____

_____

_____

_____

What does my family life look like now?

_____

_____

_____

_____

The three most important events this year will be:

_____

_____

_____

_____

This is one of the hard things that people don't do, and it's the first thing that I tell couples to do when they first come to us. Before you do anything else, you should sit down and have a real heart-to-heart talk about what retirement looks like for each of you and what it should be because there's nothing worse than getting to retirement to discover that you're planning on playing golf every day, and she thinks the grandkids are coming over and the two of you will take care of them every day. You need to really think about those things ahead of schedule, and most people don't. You may assume that you know what your spouse is going to say, but based on what I've seen, you probably don't. That's why it's important to get specific, to be

SURVIVING THE PERFECT STORM

honest, and to compare notes. Because the fact of the matter is that life changes once you go from employed/parenting/busy to retired/ empty nest/leisure. And you've both been so busy getting it all done that chances are that you've lost track a little bit.

Retirement changes things. For one, we have a spouse in the house, who we realize we're not used to spending a lot of time with. When we are home all day in retirement, we will be spending a lot more time with that person. If you think about it, most of us work forty, maybe even fifty, hours a week. Then we have activities with friends or our children. Our spouse has the same kind of schedule, so we see our spouse maybe a couple of hours in the evening, in which case we're busy helping the kids with homework, cooking dinner, paying bills, cleaning, fixing, repairing, and doing "stuff." We have free time on the weekends, but frequently even those days are filled with family responsibilities – again, we're busy doing "stuff." That two-week vacation a year is probably the only opportunity we have to spend any type of serious one-on-one time. Too often it's not until we're on the verge of retirement that we realize, "Hey, I'm going to be spending a lot of time with this person," and that shift to 24/7 togetherness starts to come into focus. It's a worthwhile exercise to begin to get reacquainted, especially when you're talking about how you're going to spend the rest of your lives together.

Another important exercise involves accepting the fact that, despite what you think to the contrary, your spending in retirement will probably mirror your spending now, for at least the first ten to twenty years. Look honestly at your current budget. If you're spending $1,000 a month now, you'll probably spend the same in retirement. Track your bills over thirty days. How often do you hit the ATM? What about Starbucks in the morning? Again, this is something that each of you needs to do. Then compare notes. This has to be an open dialogue with no pointed fingers.

The next step is to add up those regular, predictable, unavoidable expenses that hit you every month. What does your budget look like? Use these tools to help create one you can live with and within. Please visit www.primefs.com for additional budgeting tools.

Monthly Amount

Total Income $

Salary/Wages (Husband)	
Less 401(k)/Retirement Plan Contr.	
Less Taxes Withheld	
Less Other Deductions	
NET Salary/Wages (Husband)	
Salary/Wages (Wife)	
Less 401(k)/Retirement Plan Contr.	
Less Taxes Withheld	
Less Other Deductions	
NET Salary/Wages (Wife)	

Over Budget

Total Spending: $

Transportation $

- Auto Loan/Lease
- Insurance
- Husband's train pass
- Wife's Metro pass
- Registration/Inspection
- Gas
- Maintenance
- Other

Home $

- Mortgage
- Rent
- Maintenance
- Insurance
- Furniture
- Household Supplies
- Groceries
- Real Estate Tax
- Other
- Other
- Other

Utilities $

- Phone - Home
- Phone - Cell
- Cable
- Gas
- Water
- Electricity
- Internet
- Other

Health $

- Dental
- Medical
- Medication
- Vision/contacts
- Life Insurance
- Other
- Other

Entertainment $

- Memberships
- Dining out
- Events
- Subscriptions
- Movies
- Music
- Hobbies
- Travel/ Vacation
- Other
- Other

Miscellaneous $

- Dry Cleaning
- New Clothes
- Donations
- Child Care
- Tuition
- College Loans
- Pocket Money
- Gifts
- Credit Card
- Other
- Other
- Other

Too often when we're trying to put the numbers down, we look at our checkbook or our credit card statement and say, "Okay, here are the numbers. I wrote a check for this. I wrote a check for that. This was direct pay, that was direct pay, and this was direct pay. Therefore, my bills are …" But if that's how you do your budget, you're going to come up short because you didn't include your $5 cup of coffee every morning. You didn't include lunch with your kids. You didn't include all those little things that we nickel and dime and don't really track accurately because they aren't things for which we write a regular check or have on autopay. So often, people come in with their budget worksheets, and I say, "Okay, what do you guys do for meals and entertainment?" and they'll tell me, "Oh, I don't know. Maybe fifty bucks a month."

I know they're wrong, and I tell them, "No, that can't be right. You mean to tell me you do two lunches a month at McDonalds? Because that's fifty bucks." That's all you do for entertainment? You never go see a movie? You never go to a concert? You never go to the theater?

You need to include all those other little things that you do on a day-to-day basis to make sure that you've incorporated all of the spending that you're going to have. Once you've done that, then you can really start the process of figuring out whether you have enough money, which is where we'll go in the next chapter.

MIKE'S BOTTOM LINE

Have the talk with your spouse. Figure out what you need. Figure out what you want above and beyond that, and don't forget the little extras that add up.

CHAPTER THREE

HOW MUCH
IS ENOUGH?

To answer the question of whether you have enough money, first we need to ask whether you are going to have a pension.

If you have a pension, did you elect survivor benefits? That means that if you are collecting benefits, typically you are allowed to make the election that when you die, your spouse gets some percentage of your pension. In exchange for that, you take less up front. By way of example, your pension might be $2,000 a month if you chose not to take that survivor benefit. But if you want your spouse to get $1,000 a month in the event of your death, you'll only get to take $1,850 today, instead of $2,000.

You need to decide whether you're going to make that election and whether it makes better sense to buy a life insurance policy to supplement the surviving spouse's income rather than take a reduced amount. For example, take that $2,000 pension. If you were to take $150 a month out of that $2,000, thereby getting the same $1,850 as a spousal election, how much life insurance can you buy for that $150 a month? If that will cover enough life insurance to protect your spouse, then maybe it makes sense to take the full pension instead of the survivor benefit because if your spouse predeceases you, you may be stuck at $1,850, whereas if you've taken the life insurance instead and your spouse dies first, you can stop paying for the life insurance policy and get an immediate raise back up to $2,000.

Survivorship Pension?

50% Survivorship Pension along with loss of spouse's social security? We call that moving to a new neighborhood.

Because there are so many variations of a spousal election, it sometimes makes sense to sit down with somebody and do the math on how each of these elections is going to work. Keep in mind that frequently, in order to maintain health benefits for the surviving spouse, you have to elect some sort of spousal benefit.

For example, if you work for the federal government and you're under the old retirement system, CSRS, if you do not elect a survivorship benefit for your spouse and you pass away, the medical benefit passes away with you. Leaving your spouse without medical coverage is a terrible idea unless your spouse has it from another source.

The other thing that you need to take into consideration is Social Security because despite the political and financial questions we're faced with concerning its ultimate viability, Social Security will be there in some shape or form. It might be adjusted. For instance, it might become needs based. It's possible too that the age at which it becomes available to you will change from its current level. When to collect it is something you'll have to look carefully at because the age at which you begin claiming benefits affects your monthly check.

If you are in your forties to fifties, do you want to assume that the full amount will be available to you, or should you assume that there will be a reduction in your Social Security income? Sometimes it's better to assume you're not ultimately going to have 100 percent. That way, you may have more than you need. If you assume that you will have 100 percent, and the government makes some sort of modification, you wind up with less. Going forward, given the fiscal problems that we're having in this decade and given the political climate, it might make sense to underestimate your Social Security. Take a look at your most recent Social Security statement and you'll see in writing that the Social Security Administration (SSA) says it may not have enough money to pay you during you retirement years – just another reason you may want to plan accordingly.

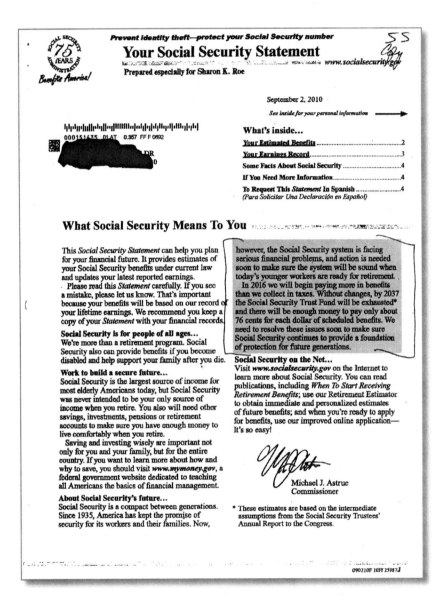

Another aspect of Social Security that you need to clearly and thoroughly understand are the options on how to take it and when to take it, especially if there's an age difference between you and your spouse. People automatically assume that the husband takes his based on his income, and the wife takes hers based on her income, unless

50 percent of his benefit is more than her total benefit, in which case she claims the spousal benefit based on his instead.

For example, let's say that the wife is sixty-two years of age and her husband is sixty-six. His full Social Security benefit is $2,000 a month. Because she was a stay-at-home mom while the kids were young, the wife hadn't had as many peak earning years, so her Social Security benefit at age sixty-two is $665. She can elect to take her $665, or she can take 35% of his, which would be $700. Which would you choose?

Most people would say, "I want the $700." But if, instead of taking $700 now, she waits until she hits her full retirement age of sixty-six, she would then be able to claim a monthly benefit of $950 (which is her full Social Security benefit) or 50% of his, which would be $1,000. She can take her spousal benefit of $1,000 now, based on 50% of his benefit, and 4 years later, at age 70, change back to her own retirement benefit and she gets a significant increase, all the way up to $1,254. And that doesn't even count COLA's. Alternatively, she can just choose to take the $665 benefit she's entitled to at age sixty-two, and not get that increase later.

Then they have to compare the total they're expecting from their pensions and Social Security with how much income they need each month to live the lifestyle that they want to live. Going back to that budget, remember that it is divided into two parts, the first being the things that they have to do, mortgage payments, utilities, car payment, and so forth. Now, compare that to their I-want list: I want to play golf on Friday. I want to take the grandkids to Disney World once a year. I want to leave a legacy for my children.

Your secure, steady, predictable, reliable income should certainly cover the must-haves. You can choose to cover your I-want list with that predictable income stream, or you can choose to leave that out and hope that happenstance in the market covers that. If you happen to have enough money in your I-want account, then you can afford those extras. And if you don't happen to have enough money, then you can't.

I recommend that you plan to have the I-want list covered because the fact is that you're probably going to do those things regardless (like Adam and Sarah), and then you're going to be taking money out of one pocket to try to cover the expenses of another pocket. Rather than having a predictable income stream covering both, you would be stuck down the road when you run out of money, and that's not a good way to go. Nevertheless, you do have that choice.

So, we've figured out how much income you need, and now we have to figure out if you are short of accomplishing your goals. Let's say, using the couple above as an example, that when they did their budget with the two columns, their needs were $4,000 a month, and their wants were an additional $1,500 a month. The total predictable income stream should cover the whole $5,500 a month if they can manage it. Keep in mind this is just what they spend. They also have to account for taxes.

Top Marginal Tax Rates: 1916-2010

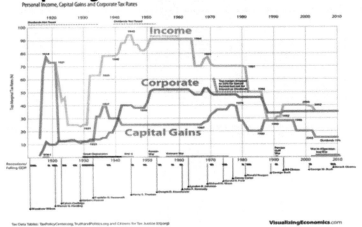

Notwithstanding all the political turmoil about which way taxes are going to go, I think that you need to minimally assume that taxes are going to go up. Again, it's better to take a conservative approach and plan for the worst. Let's assume a 28 percent tax rate between the federal and the state for this couple. Multiply that $5,500 by 1.28, and for this example and they will need $7,040 of income, so that when all's said and done they will have $5,500 to spend after covering federal and state taxes.

If you move to a state without state taxes, then of course you can drop your tax rates down appropriately. Also keep in mind that some states do not tax pension and/or Social Security income, so you can figure that into the equation too. If your income stream is large enough to put you into a higher tax bracket, you need to base your calculations on that. You can go to the IRS website (www.irs. gov) and get the tax rates for your income level so that you can plan accordingly.

Now, we know how much income the couple will need. In this situation it's $7,040. The husband's pension is $2,000. He's getting $2,000 for his Social Security and they elected $1,000 for her Social Security, so, at this point they have an income of $5,000, putting them $2,040 short of the mark. That money needs to come out of the assets they've saved, the money from 401(k)s, 403(b)s, their TSPs, their 457s, or whatever savings vehicle they have. Their retirement plans have to produce this income.

There are a couple of schools of thought on how to do this. The T. Rowe Price or the Vanguard websites run what are called Monte Carlo simulations, which let you know, if you have an investment allocation of a certain ratio, whether you can meet your retirement expectations. For example, if the couple has 75 percent of their money in equities and 25 percent in fixed income, and they need to draw out $2,040 a month, the websites can tell them what their percentage chance is of accomplishing that. Obviously, the more money they start with, the greater opportunity for success, but in general what they're looking at is somewhere in the neighborhood of a 2 to 5 percent withdrawal rate to be successful. That is, they can withdraw somewhere between 2 and 5 percent of their investments and not worry about running out of money. However, it is called a Monte Carlo simulation and what can you do in Monte Carlo? Gamble.

In my opinion, a 2 percent withdrawal rate gives you a pretty good chance of success. A 5 percent withdrawal rate is stretching it. People often hear that the stock market produces 8 to 10 percent annual returns on average. The problem with that assumption is that it's just not true. If you look at 2000 to 2010, the market certainly did not produce 8 to 10 percent every year. Sometimes the market is up 14 percent for the year, but for others it's down 14 percent. Look at 2008. The market was down between 40 and 50 percent. You can't assume that every year your nest egg is going to grow at a steady 8 or 10 percent. You have to take the volatility into account, which is what a Monte Carlo simulator does. In effect, it spins a roulette wheel and says what your return is on a given day. Then it spins it for every single day of the year and averages that out. Sometimes it does really well. Sometimes it does really poorly, but it takes fluctuations into account. That gives us a better feel for what the market is likely to do over time. The emphasis is on "feel."

I mentioned in prior chapters the whole idea of sequence of returns, and this is where it becomes so important to understand a predictable income stream. If you're leaving your money in the stock market in any way, shape or form – and I don't care if it's 50 percent equity/50 percent fixed, or 75 percent equity/25 percent fixed – you're subject to the volatility of the market. And if you're withdrawing money in a downward trend of the stock market, statistically you are going to run short of money.

Sequence of Returns: Can Work For You or Against You

5% Withdrawals Begin at Age 62	Hypothetical Annual Net Rate of Return	Hypothetical $250,000 Portfolio Value: Negative Returns Early	Hypothetical Annual Net Rate of Return	Hypothetical $250,000 Portfolio Value: Positive Returns Early
Beginning Value		$250,000		$250,000
62	-18.6%	$191,000	15.6%	$276,500
63	-13.8%	$151,767	6.4%	$281,321
64	-4.5%	$131,676	11.0%	$299,005
65	5.4%	$125,128	10.3%	$316,143
66	7.3%	$120,193	2.3%	$309,346
67	14.4%	$123,010	19.7%	$355,732
68	-4.0%	$103,164	2.3%	$348,988
69	6.1%	$94,084	7.8%	$360,836
70	15.9%	$93,208	8.7%	$376,394
71	5.7%	$82,211	13.3%	$410,144
72	6.2%	$70,510	8.7%	$429,028
73	10.9%	$60,892	6.2%	$438,325
74	11.1%	$49,829	13.9%	$481,430
75	7.1%	$35,010	8.1%	$502,069
76	11.0%	$19,954	-4.2%	$462,075
77	-4.2%	$0	11.0%	$493,428
78	8.1%	$0	7.1%	$508,403
79	13.9%	$0	11.1%	$544,175
80	6.2%	$0	10.9%	$582,210
81	8.7%	$0	6.2%	$596,388
82	13.3%	$0	5.7%	$607,806
83	8.7%	$0	15.9%	$681,193
84	7.8%	$0	6.1%	$698,795
85	2.3%	$0	-4.0%	$646,173
86	19.7%	$0	14.4%	$713,812
87	2.3%	$0	7.3%	$739,748
88	10.3%	$0	5.4%	$752,737
89	11.0%	$0	-4.5%	$691,098
90	6.4%	$0	-13.8%	$567,127
91	15.6%	$0	-18.6%	$432,185
Average Annual Net ROR for 30-year period	6.0%	Negative returns early deplete savings after 15 years	6.0%	Positive returns early can extend savings more than 30 years despite the same average annual net rate of return

By way of example, if you had $1 million in 2000, and you were taking out $40,000 a year, you'd have run out of money by 2010 because every time the market dropped, you had to sell more and more shares just to produce the same $40,000. A 4 percent withdrawal rate for most people seems reasonable, except that in the first year when you withdrew $40,000, the market dropped 25 percent. Then the next year you withdrew $40,000, and the market dropped another 25 percent. The third year you withdrew $40,000, and the market dropped 20 percent. You had three years in a row of these horrific markets, and between market losses and withdrawals your investments are worth slightly less than $500,000. By 2003 when the market started to turn back around, instead of having withdrawn only $120,000, or $40,000 times three, you are drawing $40,000 on a portfolio valued at about $500,000. To maintain your $40,000 withdrawals, you have to take slightly more than 8 percent from your accounts. A portfolio can't sustain an 8 percent withdrawal rate for very long.

If you had a crystal ball and you knew the stock market was going to go up, obviously you'd have your money there. And if you looked at that same crystal ball and knew the market was going to go down, obviously you would take your money out of the stock market.

Unfortunately, we don't have a crystal ball. Rather than hoping and praying that things go up instead of up, down, and sideways as they've done over the years, it makes better sense to have a safe, steady, reliable, and predictable income stream. And you do that by using sixth-grade math. Here's a rate of return that you know you can get. It's a guaranteed rate of return. It's going to produce this much money, and at the end of the term it's going to be a fixed number. Then you can start taking out X amount of money from a fixed number that doesn't go up or down with the stock market.

Fortunately, there are places you can go to find "safe" money. We'll discuss that in the next chapter.

MIKE'S BOTTOM LINE

Take ONLY the risk that you have to take in order to accomplish your retirement goals. Step away from the stock market retirement roller coaster.

CHAPTER FOUR

THE RULES OF MONEY

Where should you invest your money in order to get the returns that you're looking for? There are really only a couple of places to go – and I don't care if you're doing this on your own or with a financial advisor, a stockbroker, or an insurance salesman. There are only three worlds of money where you can invest your money, and they're available to all of us.

I find that people are always looking for three things: They're looking for safety; they're looking for growth; and they're looking for liquidity. But here's the deal: You get to pick only two out of three. You can't have all three of them. So you're going to sacrifice one thing for the other two. It is the proverbial "can't have your cake and eat it too."

People who are looking for safety have three places to go in terms of investment. One is a bank. Why are banks safe? Well, they offer

CDs, money market accounts, and savings accounts, and they're all FDIC-insured. We feel very comfortable with FDIC insurance, although I think that there's enough evidence to suggest that the FDIC isn't as financially secure as we might think.

Federal Deposit
Insurance Corporation
Each Depositor Insured to at least $250,000 per insured bank.

FDIC Announces Updated Deposit Insurance Fund Loss and Reserve Ratio Projections
Projects Positive Fund by This Year April 12, 2011

"....While these loss projections are subject to considerable uncertainty, under these projections and current assessment rates, the fund should become positive this year and reach 1.15 percent of estimated insured deposits in 2018."

"....expect an 11% default rate ....."

http://www.fdic.gov/news/news/press/2011/pr11066.html

The second place you can go for what constitutes safe money is the federal government, which issues all sorts of bonds, including treasuries and EE bonds. Again, we feel safe with them because they're backed by the full faith and credit of the United States Government. If you think about the huge financial meltdown of 2008, the federal government was offering three- to six-month treasuries that paid zero interest. Basically, the government was saying, "Listen, give us your money. Let us use it for ninety days, and we'll give it back to you. We're not going to pay you anything for the use of that money, but we'll give it back to you ninety days later," and people flocked to them because they were afraid of the markets.

The third place you can go to is to an insurance company, which offers something called a fixed annuity. A fixed annuity smells and looks a lot like a CD. Typically over five years the insurance company will offer you a fixed rate of return in exchange for using your money. You give the company X amount, and it gives you a contract that says, "In Y amount of time from now, you're going to earn this much interest." The major difference is that a CD is insured by the FDIC, and a fixed annuity is insured by the claims-paying ability of the issuing insurance company.

These three investment sources – the federal government, banks, and the insurance companies – have three things in common: One, all three guarantee your principle. The guarantee goes beyond just, "We promise the money will be there, and you can walk away with it." That's an important feature. They are all contractually bound to pay you back your principal, and we can't say that about a mutual fund or stock. The second thing that they all guarantee is an interest rate. It might not be the rate an investor desires, but it is guaranteed. The third thing they have in common is that in each case there are some strings attached to that money, and this goes to that liquidity issue. They all have penalties or potential loss of principal with early withdrawal. If you buy a five-year CD and you cash it out in three years, you're going to suffer a penalty in the form of lost interest. If you buy a ten-year treasury, and you sell it in three years, it's very likely that you'll get less money back on your sale than what you paid for the treasury in the first place. If you buy a five-year fixed annuity and you cash that in after three years, you're going to pay some sort of surrender charge. Minimally, you will lose interest, just like your CD.

Historically, they tell us that these fixed products pay interest somewhere between 2 and 5 percent, and certainly over the last ten years, since the '80s and '90s, that's probably been true. We've seen an average of about 2 to 5 percent over that time period, but recently the interest rates have been horrific. Right now, a five-year CD is paying 2 percent if you're lucky. But if you're looking strictly for safety, then using a fixed-rate investment is a possibility.

Where can you go for growth? It could be to a mutual fund family, for instance, T. Rowe Price, Vanguard, Oppenheimer, or American Funds. If you were to call one of these fund families up and say, "I have $100,000 of retirement money to invest," they're going to tell you to buy their mutual funds. All of these funds have costs associated with them, so it's important that you understand the fees that you'd pay. There's a *Wall Street Journal* article titled "The Hidden Cost of Mutual Funds," from April 2009, that explains that the average management fee for a mutual fund is 1.4 percent, and average trading costs are 1.1 percent. You don't necessarily see those trading costs. People often think that their mutual fund costs them 0.5 percent to own, but frequently it turns out to be more like 1.5 to 2 percent. Buyers don't understand the trading costs because they're not clearly disclosed and explained. As an aside, that is one of the advantages of working with a fee-based planner like us: You see your fees.

A second place you can go to invest if you want growth is a brokerage firm. Brokers will sell you stocks, bonds, mutual funds – whatever the flavor of the month is. Depending on the brokerage and what it's pushing at that point, those suggestions can be great or not so great. And I want to point out that stock brokers are probably the best salesmen out there today. Think about it: they convince retirees to take 100 percent of their life savings and invest that money in a vehicle in which the retirees know they could lose 100 percent of those hard-earned dollars. Those are truly great salesmen.

Alternatively, you can also go to an insurance company that offers a variable annuity. With this, you're invested in the stock market. Your money goes up and down just as the stock market does, and it's invested in what are called subaccounts. These subaccounts aren't exactly like mutual funds, but they smell and act a lot like a mutual fund.

These three growth groups have three important things in common. First and foremost, there's no guarantee that your principal will remain intact and that you can walk away with that principal down the road. Second, there's no guarantee that you're going to make money or that you can walk away with that money, and third, as we've heard over and over again from the experts, invest in the stock market for the long haul. The reason that they say "for the long haul" is because they know in the short term the market is very volatile, so time needs to be on your side. They tell us stock market growth should average somewhere in the neighborhood of 8 to 12 percent, and certainly if you're going to risk losing 20 to 50 percent, as many people did in 2008, you should make 8 to 12 percent when the markets are performing well. Keep in mind, most advisors say if you're going to invest in the stock market you should not count on using this money for at least seven to ten years. And remember, just

SURVIVING THE PERFECT STORM

like CDs, treasuries, and fixed annuities, you must understand the fees and charges associated with these types of investments.

In the big scheme of things we have to understand that in these worlds of money, all parties are fighting over the same dollar: our dollar. Banks, insurance companies, and mutual fund companies all want us to give our money to them to invest and hold for us. They want to use our money for their purposes, and they'll "share the wealth," or lack thereof, in some instances. Because of that, and because I believe that banks and insurance companies don't like to share their toys, they created a third world of investments, which we call hybrid investments. These share a little bit of the features of safety and growth. Insurance companies came out with equity-linked index annuities. Banks, seeing the opportunity and wanting to compete for the same dollars, jumped in with equity-linked CDs.

Here's how these hybrids work. Both of them start with the notion of safety, by guaranteeing your principal. The FDIC insures CDs, and index annuities are insured by the claims-paying ability of insurance companies, so in both cases your principal is guaranteed. You are guaranteed some nominal interest rate, which varies by contract. Both the annuity and the CD offer an indirect link to the equities market. The way this works is that in exchange for taking your money and promising you won't lose any of your principal, they cap your upside exposure. So, for example, an equity index annuity might have a cap of 5 percent, which means that even if the stock market goes up 30 percent you're going to get a 5 percent return. If the stock market goes up 10 percent, you go up 5 percent. If the stock market goes up 3 percent, you go up 3 percent. But here's the important part: If the stock market goes *down* 20 percent, you go up whatever that nominal interest rate is, so even if the stock market goes down 3 percent, you go up the contractually bound interest rate. But the most important part of these two products is that your principal remains intact. It never goes backward.

There may be various moving parts – the caps and participation might change from contract to contract, and some of them might have other riders on them – but the underlying concept remains consistent in that: one, your principal is guaranteed; two, you're guaranteed to earn some interest; and three, just like all the other safety-world money, if you take it out early, you'll be charged a penalty because you are buying into this thing for a longer-term investment.

We refer to these options as the world of money.

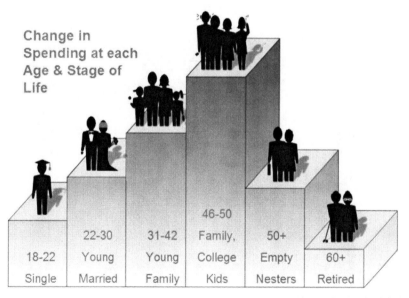

Copyright HS Dent 2009

There's a great report from the University of Pennsylvania's Wharton School of Business by lead author David Babbel: the Wharton Financial Institutions Center's *Personal Finance Real-World Index Annuity Returns*, revised December 27, 2010. This report is interesting in that wasn't produced or paid for by an insurance company, bank, or by a mutual fund company. In it, the authors analyzed returns from the various types of annuity over ten years and showed that from a risk-return standpoint, index annuities might be a viable tool for some people who want safety with the potential of a little bit more growth than they might otherwise get with a CD or a fixed annuity. We have choices of which of these or which combination of these to use, but the important part to remember is that between safety, growth, and liquidity, you get to pick two.

I Don't Have a Crystal Ball But I Can Do the Math

5 Year Annualized Returns: 1997- 2007

1. Taxable Bond Mutual Funds   **5.39%**

2. Fixed Annuities   **4.73%**

3. 1 Year CD Rate Average   **5.2%**

4. Fixed Indexed Annuities   **5.79%**

5. S&P 500   **3.61%**

Wharton Financial Institutions Center. Real World Index Annuity Returns. March 4, 2010.

Once we understand how much we need and where we can invest our money, we have to figure out how much we should invest in any particular area. I like to use the "bucket" approach for income planning. One bucket is invested in such a way as to create the necessary income for the first five years of retirement. The second is invested for years six through ten, and a third bucket covers the remainder of retirement. Below is an example of how this might work.

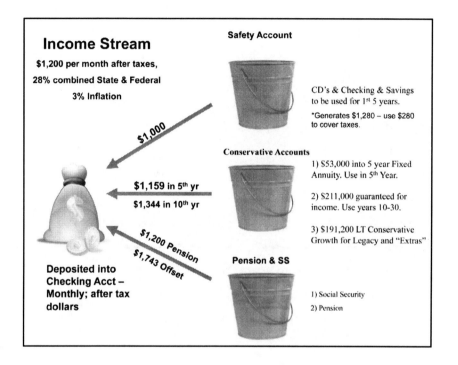

Income Stream

$1,200 per month after taxes,
28% combined State & Federal
3% Inflation

$1,000

$1,159 in 5th yr
$1,344 in 10th yr

$1,200 Pension
$1,743 Offset

Deposited into
Checking Acct –
Monthly; after tax
dollars

Safety Account

CD's & Checking & Savings
to be used for 1st 5 years.
*Generates $1,280 – use $280
to cover taxes.

Conservative Accounts

1) $53,000 into 5 year Fixed
Annuity. Use in 5th Year.

2) $211,000 guaranteed for
income. Use years 10-30.

3) $191,200 LT Conservative
Growth for Legacy and "Extras"

Pension & SS

1) Social Security
2) Pension

What we always do when we're designing an income string for our retirees is to begin with the first bucket, which is the money that they're going to use during the first five years. That money is almost always from the world of safety, so traditionally we use money-market CDs and perhaps treasuries because they offer safety and the most liquidity in the world of safe money. This way, we take away the whole concern of the sequence of returns, which, as you'll recall, has to do with taking withdrawals from your investment accounts when the stock market's on a downward trend, forcing you to sell more and more shares to come up with the same dollar amount for your income needs. We take that risk completely off the table because investors take money out of fixed income accounts, which means their money's stable. It's not sexy. It's not glamorous. At a cocktail party when all your friends are talking about their 20 percent return from the market, you're not having that conversation, but remember, all those friends who talked about how well they did when the market was up don't mention that they lost 30 percent when the market went down. Take yourself out of that conversation. There's no reason to be stressed during retirement, worrying about what the market might do.

For the first five years, we think that using laddered CDs, money markets, and perhaps treasuries is the safest, most secure way to guarantee your income stream. For your second bucket, years six through ten, we typically use a fixed annuity, which pays a little bit better interest rate than a CD. There are fixed amounts you'll need to put into these to assure the income stream you need, and inflation always needs to be factored in. Your third bucket is designed to produce income for years eleven through thirty. We always plan out to ages ninety to ninety-five because I'd rather have too much and not need it than come up short, and going back to work at age eighty-seven should not be a part of anybody's plan. For this bucket, we strongly recommend either an index annuity with a living benefit rider or a variable annuity with a living benefit rider. I prefer an index annuity with a living benefit rider because it's straight-up math. Investors know what the number's going to be, and if something catastrophic happens in the meantime and you want to walk away with money, you know you'll walk away with your principal at a minimum. A variable annuity goes up and down with the stock market, so your principal could disappear, and you don't want to be in that position down the road.

It's important to keep in mind two key points: First and foremost, surrender charges may apply, which may reduce your principal, and second, the living benefits concept can be very convoluted, and they vary from contract to contract, so you certainly have to sit down with a professional who can help you to understand how they work. Because you're dealing with an insurance company, it will guarantee you an income stream for your life and, if you elect, the life of your surviving spouse. The carrot that insurance companies dangle is the guarantee that your principal is going to grow by a specified contractual rate.

For an example, as of the writing of this book, there are several contractually bound companies offering contracts that guarantee your principle will grow by 8 percent. These numbers compound, and we all understand the power of compounding, but keep in mind this guaranteed growth rate. That is not walk-away money. It is to be used strictly as income. You get to withdraw that money a little at a time over the course of your life, and over the course of your surviving spouse's life. Think about this guaranteed growth money as being more like a pension. It's going to turn into an income stream. You worked all your life, and every two weeks you got a paycheck. An index annuity with a living benefit rider will create a retirement paycheck for you.

If you have money left over after filling your retirement income buckets, go ahead and invest in equities. Risk is acceptable when you know that everything you require to live is already paid for.

A caveat on using any investment vehicle – there are always strings attached. Make sure you understand what strings are attached to your retirement strategies and investments. Consider the following:

Strings Attached

There Are Strings Attached to **ALL** Investments:
- Fees
- Surrender Charges
- Liquidity
- Credit Worthiness
- Market Risk
- Interest Rate Risk
- Taxes
- More?????

Know What Strings Are Attached to Your Investments
Trust Your Gut Reaction
Speak to a Professional

MIKE'S BOTTOM LINE

Make sure you've filled the three buckets that will fund your retirement with the right low- or no-risk investments to guarantee a safe and worry-free retirement and don't forget to factor in inflation.

CHAPTER FIVE

SMART ESTATE PLANNING

N ow that you've made a plan to secure your income, the next most important step to safeguarding your retirement is securing your estate and providing for the well-being of your surviving spouse and heirs. That starts with a good, sound estate plan. There are three basic tools that every person must have – and I do mean must. You must have an advanced care directive; you must have a power of attorney for financial matters; and you *must* have a will.

You can choose to do other estate planning that involves the use of trusts: an irrevocable life insurance trust, a Medicaid planning trust, a generation-skipping trust, a charitable remainder trust, a grantor trust (one of my favorites because it allows you to qualify for Medicaid and still maintain control over the assets), and a legacy trust. There are all sorts of trusts out there that you can use that have some wonderful benefits to you and your family, but before you do anything else, secure those three key documents: the will, the advanced care directive, and the financial power of attorney.

The Final Blow – Death & Taxes

Federal & State Death Taxes
    State   10 -16%
    Federal 37-55%

Probate Avoidance
- Transfer on Death Accounts
- Beneficiary Designations
- Trusts

Most Powerful Tool

Advance Care Directive & Power of Attorney for Financial Matters

Let's look at the advanced care directive first. This is broken into two parts. The first is the medical directive, which deals with how and by whom day-to-day medical decisions will be made for you when you're no longer able or willing to do so. This includes whether or not you're going into a nursing home, what medications you take, and what type of treatment plans you should be following. Day-to-day medical decisions inevitably need to be made, and at some point you may not be able to make those decisions, so you need to appoint somebody to make them on your behalf. Typically it would be your spouse and/or your children, but it could be a close friend or a close relative, keeping in mind that it might make sense to have somebody a little bit younger than yourself, since your contemporaries may well have the same kinds of issues facing them when this directive takes effect. An important thing to note here is that an advanced care directive comes into play only when two doctors, or a judge, or a court, determine that you can no longer make the decisions on your own, or when you acknowledge that. In no way does it mean that you've relinquished your control as soon as you sign it.

The second part of the advanced directive is the living will. The laws on these vary from state to state, but the basic tenets of the living will are to decide – if you should be in a persistent vegetative state, or a terminal condition, or if your doctors judge you to be at the end of your life – whether you want all measures used to continue your life, or do you want the proverbial plug pulled? It's a personal choice that you should discuss with your family, but it should be in writing, less because of the legal issues and more because you're giving your family direction on what it is you want done. You may think that you've covered this in a conversation with your spouse or children, but you're risking putting them in a heartbreaking situation if they're called upon to decide when to let you go. Take that burden away from them. Put it in writing and tell them what to do. There's always this fear that if you sign a living will that says you don't want extraordinary measures taken, somebody's going to show up and just pull the plug on you, but that's not how it works.

A good example of this is my father-in-law. A couple of years ago he slipped and fell and hurt his hip. When he fell and hurt himself, they took him to the hospital where he was given pain medication. He had a violent allergic reaction to the pain medication they gave him. He was hallucinating and became very agitated and violent. In order to control the reaction so they could treat his hip, the doctors put him into an induced coma. The doctors knew this was temporary fix to a temporary problem and that as soon as the effects of the drug were out of his system they would pull him out of that coma, so there was no question of his wife being able to say, "Pull the plug."

The second tool is a little bit more slippery. It's called the power of attorney for financial matters. This is always an intimidating document because in most states it becomes effective as soon as you sign it. This document gives authority to another person – again, typically your spouse and a trusted family member – to make financial decisions for you. Anything that requires your signature, anything that requires your approval, this financial power of attorney makes it possible for the person or people named in it to do on your behalf.

Why would you do this? Well, let's say that you're the primary breadwinner in your marriage, and this was the husband in the generation we're talking about. Your name is on the car, the house, and everything else that you and your wife own. Your retirement money is in your 401(k), not in hers. Now, what happens if you have a stroke, or are in a car accident, and can no longer make financial decisions on your own? Your wife can't sell your home to accommodate your disabilities because your name is on the deed with hers. She can't contact your broker or your bank and take money from your retirement accounts to support you both because she hasn't got the authority. She can't even get rid of your car.

This financial power of attorney takes care of all that and grants whomever you've named the ability to act on your behalf. They have what's called a fiduciary duty, which means they have to do what's in your best interest. Unfortunately, a significant number of states do not have criminal sanctions for people who violate their fiduciary duty. They have civil sanctions, which means if you give this power to somebody who abuses it, the only recourse most of us have would be a civil suit against the person, not criminal charges. That said, this financial power of attorney is still a necessary evil because the result of NOT having one in place can be catastrophic. If your wife can't get into your 401(k), how does she pay your bills? How does she get Social Security when you turn sixty-two years of age or become disabled? She can't do anything without that power of attorney. Her only alternative is to go to court and get guardianship, but that's even worse. She has to hire an attorney to represent her in order to get permission from the court to take care of you, and additionally she has to hire an attorney for you, to protect you from her taking care of you. Then, every year she has to report to the court exactly where she spent every penny of your money, and court reporting is onerous. She would have to account for every penny. If she spends $20 on Depends, it has to be reported. If she spends money on doctor bills or daycare, every single penny has to be reported. That's a huge, huge task, and that's why you need to assign that financial power of attorney. Even though it may make you feel uneasy, the alternatives are so much worse for your spouse and family.

Last but not least of the documents that you must have is a will. The will is a document that allows us to transfer the items that we own to another person after we've died. Think about it from this perspective: If you own a vehicle, it's registered with the state, and if you want to sell that vehicle or give it to somebody else, you have to sign on the back of your title to transfer the asset to another party. If you're dead, who signs the back of that title? Your personal representative or your executor would do that, and the executor is appointed by the will. The will traditionally says something like, "I love my spouse. Give it all to him or her, and if she's not there, give it to my kids."

What are some of the other important topics covered in a will? If you have minor children, it might make sense that when you pass away, a sixteen-year-old son or daughter does not inherit all your money because he or she would be insufficiently mature to handle it responsibly. In that case, you might want to put that money into trusts for the benefit of your children so that it's doled out to them over time. The second thing that you need to consider when you're doing your will is whether you require tax planning. We hear all the time about people creating revocable living trusts to avoid tax problems, but in fact a revocable living trust does nothing toward tax savings just because it's a trust. You can do the same tax planning inside a will that you can do in a trust. It's the exact same tax language. This varies state by state, but if your estate is worth more than a certain amount, you'll want to do tax planning because otherwise an estate tax may be due.

For example, in Maryland if you die with more than $1 million of net worth, the excess greater than $1 million is subject to a 16 percent estate tax. Let's say that my wife and I have a net worth of $1.5 million. I die first, leaving a will that says, "Give the money directly to my spouse." If I give that money directly to my spouse, there's no estate tax at that time, but now she has $1.5 million to her name. Assuming that she holds on to that money until she dies, $500,000 in her estate will be subject to a 16 percent estate tax because we failed to tax-plan.

With a little bit of planning, I could have put $500,000 in trust for the benefit of my wife, which would use up my $1 million estate tax exemption. She would still have $1 million in her name, and when she passed away, the $500,000 held in trust for her from my estate would not be subject to the tax. That means that we can pass our $1.5 million to our children without any estate tax.

It's important to sit down and diagram this out with a professional. As tempted as you might be by the low price of online legal services or computer programs that generate legal documents, this is not the smart place to cut corners. Everybody's situation is unique, and because you are not an attorney and don't think of all the repercussions, you're going to check a box "yes" or "no" based on your common-sense understanding of how things work, and unfortunately the law is not common sense. Although you might want to plan your own retirement and manage your own money through retirement, creating your own estate plan is asking for disaster.

Earlier, I mentioned the uses of trusts. We all hear about using revocable living trusts to avoid probate, but what exactly is a trust? A trust is a legal document created between you and yourself, into which you transfer all your assets while you're alive. There is no tax consequence attached to the transfer of your assets from yourself to your trust. You can't transfer IRA retirement funds, but almost everything else can be transferred to this trust. The trust makes your estate easier to manage by a successor trustee. When you can't manage your affairs, somebody else can step in. It's kind of like having the president of the company running the company, and when he can no longer do so, the vice president steps up. Trusts are great for several reasons. One, they avoid probate. Avoiding probate is easy to do without creating a trust, but if you have real estate in more than one state, having a trust could make sense because in every state in which you own real property, you have to go through what's called an ancillary probate in order to transfer the assets to whomever you're trying to get them to. A trust can spare your successor trustee that necessity.

A trust can also be useful for people who have children with special needs. In this example, the definition of special needs goes beyond having a handicap or a disability. It can also be a substance abuse problem or it could be because, much to your chagrin, your child's an idiot (none of us have children with the intent that they should turn out to be idiots, but we all encounter them, and somebody produced that kid). A trust can protect these children. Your estate can be held in trust and set up to dole out money to them so that they can't just access the money at their discretion. Money is given to them for maintenance, support, education, and health, areas that have specific legal meaning when used inside estate documents. Your trust will hold the money for them, protect them from their own shortcomings, and still provide for their support, maintenance, education, and health.

I think a trust is also a good tool when you're trying to control your money from beyond the grave. I'll use myself as an example here: When I started dating my wife in 1981, I had long hair, I had earrings, and I rode a motorcycle. I can tell you her parents were not overly excited about the prospects of their daughter dating me. Now, it's thirty years later and we're still together, so it's proved to be a good choice after all on both our parts, but at the time her parents were not thrilled about this. Added to that was that, at 18 years old, I had no concept of what money was about. But they did. My wife's father was from a prominent New England family and well off. He knew that if he left his money to my wife, at his death his money would become our money. If my wife were to die and I remarried, it might become my new wife's money, and that was not his intent. To prevent that, he put his money into trusts for my wife. She can use it to buy and sell things, but whatever she buys is owned by that trust, and when she dies that money doesn't come to me, it goes to his grandchildren. Guaranteeing that your money goes to your bloodline when you're gone is another good use of a trust.

Beneficiary designations are extremely important, which is why when clients come into my office we always review all of their documents to see who the beneficiaries are.

BENEFICIARY REVIEW
PER ACCOUNT

Account Owner's Name: _____

Type of Account: _____
IRA, Roth, SEP, 401(k), 403(b), Individual, Joint (wros)/(ten), Trust, etc

Account _____ **of** _____ **accounts**

Institution or company: _____

Account Number: _____

Balance (approximate): $ _____ as of _____ / _____ / _____

Amount of basis (after tax funds) in account or cost basis $ _____

Primary Beneficiary Should = 100%	1.	%
	2.	%
	3.	%
	4.	%
	5.	%
	Total	**%**
Contingent Beneficiary Should = 100%	1.	%
	2.	%
	3.	%
	4.	%
	5.	%
	Total	**%**

Comments: _____

_____

_____

_____

_____

_____

Advisor: Michael Canet, JD LLM   Date: _____

Contact Info: 428 North Crain Hwy

Glen Burnie, MD 21061

410-863-1040 or mcanet@primefs.com

There was recently a court case in New York that points out why. A retired schoolteacher, who'd started working at age nineteen and had lived with her parents until she was married, left an estate worth more than $1 million. She'd been married to the same man for more than fifty years when she passed, but guess whom she'd designated as her beneficiaries? Her parents! There was no contingency benefit for her husband on that account because when she'd opened it, she hadn't yet met him. Her sister was her contingent beneficiary. Her husband went all the way up to the New York Supreme Court, trying to get that money and lost all the way.

To make sure you avoid probate to the extent possible, every year you should review your legal documents to make sure that the designated beneficiaries are who you want them to be. With life insurance, typically we've listed on the policy, "When I die, give it to my spouse. When my spouse isn't there, give it to my kids." We avoid probate because we've designated beneficiaries. In most states you can designate beneficiaries on your home. You can designate beneficiaries on most bank accounts and on most investment accounts. You can designate beneficiaries on most IRAs, 401(k)s, and retirement accounts. Using this form of probate avoidance makes sense if your ultimate plan is to have the money pass to your spouse and, if he or she is not living, to your children.

The caveats to this are: One, you need to remember there are tax planning issues, and two, if you have minor children who are inheriting, leaving it to them outright via beneficiary designation might not make the best sense. You might want to do some trust planning that you can incorporate into your beneficiary designation.

What you don't want to do because it's always a disaster is to put your children on your accounts as joint owners. We see this all the time: "If something happens to me, I want my daughter's name on my account so that she can pay my bills, and when I die she'll be able to share my money directing with her siblings. That way there's no court involved, and no probate; it's just quick and easy."

All of that is correct, up to a point, but here's the problem. When her name is on that account as a joint owner, you have effectively made a gift to your daughter, which means that money is now hers as well as yours. If she can get to it, that means her creditors can get to it. If she gets in a car accident and hits somebody making $1 million a year, I guarantee you her insurance coverage does not cover lost wages because most people have coverage in the range of $250,000 to $300,000. When she gets sued by some slippery, ambulance-chasing attorney, he's smart enough to know that her name is on her parents' accounts. If she goes into bankruptcy, that's her money. If she gets divorced, depending on how slippery the divorce attorney is, it comes up in the conversation. *Do not put your children's names on your accounts.* The power of attorney allows them to pay your bills. A beneficiary designation gives it to them upon your death. That whole notion of, "Well, she can take the money and pass it out," ignores the fact that there are tax implications and credit implications for her in doing that. Don't put her in that position. The power of attorney takes care of her authority to act on the accounts on your behalf while you're alive.

MIKE'S BOTTOM LINE

The three must-have documents for estate planning are a will, an advanced care directive, and a power of attorney for financial matters. You might also want a trust. Don't go the cheap cut-and-paste-off-the-internet route because you need an attorney to review your documents to make sure they meet your specific needs.

CHAPTER SIX

LEGACY PLANNING

Once you have figured out the income needs that you'll have during retirement and allocated them to your income buckets accordingly, the next question is always, do we need to do legacy planning? For most people considering providing for their heirs – be they their children, their grandchildren, or their siblings – there are usually three schools of thought.

One is: "I worked hard for my money. I'm going to spend every bit and hopefully I'll die broke." A second is: "I'm pretty sure there's going be something left over, so probably I'll leave something for my kids." The third school of thought is: "I want to make sure my kids are taken care of when I die. I want to leave them something that will give them a foot up in life."

Starting with the easy track of spending every penny when going through retirement, plan accordingly and hope you'll be able to bounce that last check to the funeral home. If you're in the I-hope-to-leave-something-for-my-kids group, again, if you've done your planning correctly you won't deplete everything because the money has been designed to outlast you, so in that case there probably will be something left over. For most people who plan, minimally they use up their investable assets, but not their residences.

For those people in the third group, who want to leave something substantial to their kids, it's one thing to leave $5,000 or $10,000, but if they want to leave something that gives their kids a step up in life, then we're talking about a legacy that's anywhere from a couple of hundred thousand dollars to a million or more. Most people think that they're going to invest their assets in such a way that they will yield enough money to live on and that because the money will continue to grow through their retirement, there will be a substantial amount left behind. The problem with this is that it's all speculation. It's the proverbial crystal ball. You can't be sure what's going to happen. To base a legacy plan on "I hope the stock market does well" or "I hope I don't use all my money" doesn't make sense. The best way to leave a legacy is to buy a life insurance policy.

I know that your eyes are probably rolling back in your head and you're saying, "Oh, I hate life insurance. Those slimy life insurance salesmen are always tricking us into buying these products." I understand that feeling, but I also know that life insurance is a necessary evil. That's the way you approach it, just like one of those unpleasant medical exams you schedule every year. It's not comfortable. It's not enjoyable, but it's one of those things that can make a huge difference down the road.

The idea behind the life insurance is that you're going to take a portion of your assets – be it 10 percent, be it 20 percent – that you're earmarking to create a legacy plan, and the advantage of the life insurance is that it's going to create a huge multiple. Let's say for example that you are a relatively healthy seventy-year-old man or woman. You might expect to pay $60,000 a year (for ten years) toward a life insurance policy that might result in a death benefit of between $1 million and $1.5 million that is 100 percent tax-free to your heirs. Over the course of ten years, you have "invested" $600,000 into life insurance, via the yearly premiums.

Say you took that same $600,000 and invested it in another fashion, and you died twenty years later. How much will it be worth then? Is it going to be $1.5 million? It might be. Is it going to be $1 million? It might be. Could it be $100,000? Yeah, it might be. There's no certainty about how that investment will do. Life insurance gives you a way to know for certain how much money you're going to give your children. If you want to create a legacy, that's the way to do it. Plus, it is tax free. What is better for the heirs: a check for $1.5M, tax free, or a check for $900,000 of after-tax dollars ($1.5M inheritance at 40 percent tax rate – $900K going to your heirs)? Don't forget about that nasty estate tax due as well. With life insurance, you can leave it to your heirs' estate, tax and income tax free.

For a single person, at this writing, you can get a life insurance policy combined with a long-term-care policy, so that if you need the money for medical purposes, a portion is available for you. The cash value of the life insurance policy is there for you if you need it as well, so there is money available from it in an emergency, but, more important, you leave your kids this huge legacy that they'll be able to use to fund their own retirement plan.

When you buy a life insurance policy, what type should you buy? There are three basic types of life insurance. When most people think about life insurance, they consider it from one of three perspectives: One, "If I die, I need to take care of my family while I'm working."

Two, "I'll need to pay an inheritance tax bill upon my death because I have a large estate." Three, "I want to make somebody wealthy." There are life insurance policies tailored for each of these needs.

The type that best suits the need defined by "I need to take care of my family while I'm working" is called term life insurance. You buy a specified dollar amount of life insurance. You're looking to that policy to cover the expenses involved in raising your children, paying your mortgage, and supporting your surviving spouse in the event of your death. You pay a fixed premium typically for twenty to thirty years, depending on how long a period you're trying to protect your family. Once that period ends, the policy lapses. There's nothing coming back to you from that money you paid into the insurance program over those twenty years, but if you die during that time, it serves its very specific purpose.

The second type is called cash-value life insurance. This means exactly what it sounds like. I've included a chart here to illustrate how this works.

North American Company
for Life and Health Insurance
Since 1886

Executive Office
525 W. Van
Buren
Chicago, IL 60607

Custom Guarantee (Gen 6)

A Universal Life Insurance Policy Illustration

Prepared for: Agent:

Female, Age 66 (Based on Nearest Birthday), Standard Non-Tobacco
Death Benefit: $1,569,460   Initial DB Option: Level
Initial Annual Premium: $60,000.00
1035: $0.00 (Month 1) Non-1035: $0.00 (Month 1)
Riders: Chronic Illness Accelerated Benefit Rider
Rating: None

061

TABULAR DETAIL

| | | | Guaranteed 3.50% / 2.50% Interest Rate | | | Non-Guaranteed 3.50% Interest Rate | | |
End of Year	End of Yr Age	Premium Outlay	Account Value	Surrender Value	Death Benefit	Account Value	Surrender Value	Death Benefit
1	67	60000.00	19180	0	1569460	33054	0	1569460
2	68	60000.00	37090	0	1569460	65179	0	1569460
3	69	60000.00	53860	0	1569460	97507	28168	1569460
4	70	60000.00	69305	2917	1569460	130443	64055	1569460
5	71	60000.00	83411	19973	1569460	163533	100095	1569460
6	72	60000.00	95627	35140	1569460	196839	136352	1569460
7	73	60000.00	105734	48197	1569460	230101	172565	1569460
8	74	60000.00	113496	58911	1569460	262756	208170	1569460
9	75	60000.00	118308	65935	1569460	294724	242351	1569460
10	76	60000.00	119867	70444	1569460	325781	276359	1569460
11	77	0.00	66980	20509	1569460	305544	259072	1569460
12	78	0.00	6627	0	1569460	281294	238510	1569460
13	79	0.00	0	0	1569460	252543	213448	1569460
14	80	0.00	0	0	1569460	217911	182504	1569460
15	81	0.00	0	0	1569460	175812	144094	1569460
16	82	0.00	0	0	1569460	126491	98461	1569460
17	83	0.00	0	0	1569460	68238	43896	1569460
18	84	0.00	0	0	1569460	0	0	1569460
19	85	0.00	0	0	1569460	0	0	1569460
20	86	0.00	0	0	1569460	0	0	1569460
21	87	0.00	0	0	1569460	0	0	1569460
22	88	0.00	0	0	1569460	0	0	1569460
23	89	0.00	0	0	1569460	0	0	1569460
24	90	0.00	0	0	1569460	0	0	1569460
25	91	0.00	0	0	1569460	0	0	1569460

Date: 8/15/2011   State: MD   Proposal Code:34057.28CT

This is an illustration and not a contract, and is not complete without all pages.

Page 11 of 13
Version 14.3.140302 w

The underlying premise of cash-value life insurance is that as you get older insurance gets more expensive. With cash-value life insurance, you put in a consistent premium every year, and after the insurance company takes its profits, administrative costs, and expenses, the balance of your money is put in to a kind of savings account. It's called cash value because that savings grows or has the potential to grow over time.

As an example, let's say you purchase a $1.5 million plan with a premium that starts at $10,000 per year. Over time, the cost of your insurance will go up, but you'll continue to pay the same premium. The cost versus premium difference is deducted from what would have been deposited into your "savings account" cash value, so even though the cost of your premium goes up on paper, you pay a level premium.

Cash Value Life Insurance

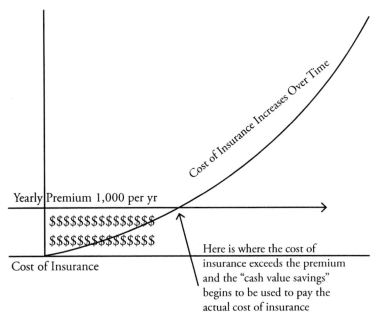

Yearly Premium 1,000 per yr

$$$$$$$$$$$$$$$$

$$$$$$$$$$$$$$$$

Cost of Insurance

Here is where the cost of insurance exceeds the premium and the "cash value savings" begins to be used to pay the actual cost of insurance

You can set the premium for a certain period of time so that the policy does not lapse, which means it's always there for your lifetime. You can pick a lifetime payment plan or a specified period of years. If you choose a lifetime approach, you will pay the premiums for your lifetime. If you choose a number of years, say ten years of payments, your premiums will be a greater, but at the end of ten years you will no longer have that payment obligation. Either way, when you pass away, that $1.5 million goes to your heirs.

How could that "savings account" you're building up grow? One way is to use something called whole-life, cash-value life insurance. This whole-life policy pays interest, and it is a fixed interest rate for the duration. Think about when you buy a CD, the interest rate typically does not change. This whole life policy will pay the same interest rate for the duration of the policy. The nice thing about having a whole-life policy is that it's straight-up math. You know the numbers, and it's never going to go away. You don't have any mixed emotions about it when you get a statement every year because you know exactly what it's going to look like. You can actually have the insurance company run an illustration that shows the cash value from the day you start to the day you die.

Again, when your friends are sitting around the cocktail party talking about how well they're doing on their returns, you're not going to be tempted to say, "Oh, let me tell you about my cash-value life insurance policy" because it's not returning anything. Currently, the interest rate you receive on cash value life insurance might be in the 3 or 4 percent range, and in good years they might pay 5 percent.

Another possibility is a universal life policy. For all intents and purposes, it works almost exactly like a whole life policy except that the interest rate can change. I don't particularly like that because, although interest rates go up, they also go down. That means that if you're trying to leave a legacy and you assumed that the interest rates were going to remain consistently higher, but interest rates go lower, you might find yourself ten or twenty years down the road having to put more money into the policy to keep it alive. Again, remember at some point the policy starts taking money out of your "savings account" to pay the cost of insurance.

Yet another alternative is an index life. Everybody likes the sexiness of the upside of the stock market, but they hate losing money when the stock market goes down, right? Well, an index life says that if the stock market goes up, the issuer will credit your "savings account" with a percentage of the upside of the stock market. If the stock market goes down, you won't lose money, but you're not going to get that credit, either. It has the potential to do a little bit better than universal life, but it also has the potential to do a little bit worse because you might not get any interest in any given year. If you look back to our chapter on the world of money, you can review how an index policy might work.

The final option is a variable universal-life policy, which is exactly what it sounds like: It's variable. It's 100 percent invested in subaccounts. When you examine a subaccount, it looks and acts a lot like a mutual fund, so you'll hear many people make the analogy that it's basically a mutual fund at an insurance company. That means that if the stock market goes up, the value of your account goes up. If the stock market goes down, the value of your account goes down, which leaves you very exposed in a down market and leaves open the possibility that you'll have to put a lot more money into your policy down the road because the market did not do as well as you'd hoped.

For people who want to secure a known legacy for their kids, a whole life policy is probably the best way to go. The universal index is another potential option, but I would not recommend using a variable universal life because you just don't know what's going to happen. A variable universal life is great for people who have fully funded their retirement accounts and still have excess money that they want to grow tax deferred. In that situation, a variable universal life might be an appropriate tool. But for legacy planning, I prefer the other three.

Let's talk about some of the nuances of how cash-value life insurance works. There are some tax code sections that say that as that cash value grows, you do not pay tax on it, which is nice. The other thing the tax code sections allow you to do is to borrow out the growth in the account. For example, if you put $100,000 into it and, because of interest rates or stock market returns, it's grown to $200,000, the tax code allows you to borrow that $100,000, and you do not pay tax on borrowed money. That's a way to get tax-free income. In addition, if you need to or want to, there are also provisions that allow you to take back your principal. Again, whenever you're using your own principal, there are no tax consequences. The caveat to all this is that if you do it incorrectly, you could collapse the life insurance policy and wind up with a huge tax bill. So, before you start drawing money out of a cash-value life insurance policy, make sure you talk to a professional so that you understand what the tax implications might be.

The next question to consider in setting up a life insurance policy for the benefit of your children is how you want them to receive that benefit. Do you want the insurance money paid directly to them, or do you want it doled out in a way that will encourage them to be responsible with it? Another issue that you need to think through is that the death benefit of life insurance is taxable for estate and inheritance tax purposes. It's income-tax free to the beneficiaries, but it may cause a taxable event to your estate. If you've purchased a $1.5 million life insurance policy for the benefit of your children and you happen to reside in a state such as Maryland, which taxes your estate 16 percent on assets greater than $1 million, all of a sudden you've created an $80,000 estate tax bill. That can be easily avoided by using a life insurance trust. There are various versions of how a life insurance trust can be used, and you'd be wise to talk to an attorney when you set one of these up. The basic idea behind a life insurance trust is that when you create a life insurance trust and buy a life insurance policy, you can either buy it inside the trust, meaning you've already created the trust before you buy the life insurance policy, or you can buy a life insurance policy, set up the trust, and then transfer the life insurance policy to the trust. There are estate tax implications called a "look-back period" to transferring an existing life insurance policy to the trust. If you die within five years of transferring the life insurance policy to the trust, the federal government will say it was a gift that was not completed in time and it will be included in your estate for estate-tax purposes. While you do need to take that into consideration, most people doing this legacy planning are between sixty-five and seventy-five years old, and more likely than not they'll live longer than that five years, so transferring the life insurance to the trust after purchasing it is still workable.

There are very strict guidelines on how you interact with the trust because essentially what you're doing every year in paying that premium is making a gift to the beneficiaries of the trust. When you put the money into this trust account, the trustee sends the children a letter saying, "Your parents have made a gift to this trust to use for life insurance premiums. You have thirty days to decide whether you want to take the money or let it be used for life insurance premiums." It's called a "Crummey Letter," named after a doctor in San Francisco.

Parents sometimes get a little bit nervous about this. "I have to put the premium in there, and my kids have thirty days in which they have the option to take it?" Yep, it's part of the rules, and here's the deal: If one of your kids takes his or her portion of the premium that you've put in, cut the kid off. Change the policy and say, "Fine. You're not going to get the life insurance policy because you're taking your money now." Most kids are not going to take that $10,000 or $5,000. They want their $750,000 when you pass.

You do have to follow some rules when it comes to using a life insurance trust, but here's the benefit of it: Once you've established this trust and survived the look-back period, all the money coming out of it to your beneficiaries is estate-tax free and income-tax free. That is a huge advantage, especially in light of the fact that with the current economic conditions, we can expect income taxes and estate taxes to go up. Right now the federal estate tax has a $5 million exemption, so most Americans aren't subject to that tax, but don't forget that the states are trying to find sources of revenue and the estate tax is easy – dead people don't vote (except in Chicago).

The other benefit to having this trust is that you can design the distribution of the assets upon your death. At your death, this trust receives your $1.5 million, but instead of just having $750,000 distributed to each child immediately, you can set conditions. For instance, you might choose to stipulate, "Upon my death, divide the money in half: $750,000 for one child, $750,000 for another child. I want each of them to receive $100,000 immediately and then I want $250,000 of the money put into some sort of retirement annuity to guarantee them a pension at age sixty-five. The income produced from the remaining $400,000 should be distributed quarterly and they can invade the principal if needed for maintenance, support, education, and health." Alternatively, you could say, "They can take $100,000 a year for five years." There are all sorts of ways that you can control how the money comes to them. If you have any concerns about your child inheriting $750,000 that he or she might go out and blow it or not invest wisely, this is an opportunity for you to provide the continued guidance that you gave when he or she was younger. You've been through retirement. You understand all the trials and tribulations of "Do I have enough money? Am I going to make it? Here's what real medical expenses look like." Your children haven't experienced that yet, so it's not reality for them. This is a way for you to help them through that process instead of just giving them a big lump sum and letting them run with it.

To recap: If leaving a legacy for your children is important, these are the steps you need to take. You need to decide how much you want to give them upon your death. You need to decide how much of your assets you want to earmark toward that gift. Then you need to decide whether you want the money to go to them outright or whether you want to have strings attached so you can provide that guidance. You also have to decide which type of insurance vehicle you want to use. Do you want something that is reliable and predictable, or do you want something that includes some assumption of risk? Do you just want to shoot for the moon and maybe do extremely well, or maybe have to put more money into it in the event you take a loss? You need to make that decision before you start funding it.

MIKE'S BOTTOM LINE

Remember, while your home has a 1 in 2500 chance of burning down, you have 100 percent chance of dying. *Life insurance provides a safe, dependable way to leave a substantial tax-free legacy to your heirs.*

CHAPTER
SEVEN

DO YOU NEED A FINANCIAL PLANNER?

Should you be working with a financial planner? And how should you go about choosing one?

I always equate deciding whether to hire a financial planner with the experience of hiring a carpenter to build an addition on your house. You can find a carpenter who's extremely competent and can do remarkable work, but when he shows up with nothing but a hammer, a screwdriver, and a saw, it gives you pause. Does he really have the tools that are required to deliver what he's promised? I have a buddy, Phil, who can fix anything with a hammer, a saw, a screwdriver, and duct tape. But it seems to me that if you're going to be putting your financial future into someone's hands, you want somebody who shows up at your doorstep with a big ol' panel truck, maybe even with a trailer behind it, and so many tools that you can't even count them all. It's not that he's going to need every tool, but there's some comfort level in knowing that the contractor you've hired has every tool necessary to do the job.

A Truck Full of Tools

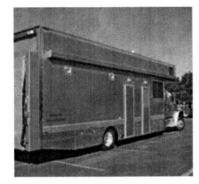

You Don't Need Every Tool for Every Job But, Better to Have Them and Know How and When to Use Them Than to Not Have Them at All.... OR WORSE YET – Not Even Know the Tool Exists!

When you're looking for a financial planner, that's what you want: somebody who has a full array of tools to take care of you. Again, it's not that the planner will necessarily need every tool, but it's better to have the tool and not need it than need the tool and not even know it exists.

A lot of people are unclear about what a financial planner is versus a financial salesman or an insurance salesman or a stockbroker. They go by various names, but it's important that when you're looking for somebody that you're clear about exactly what is it you're looking for. Are you looking for a relationship that's transaction based, one in which someone will sell you a product and then move on? In that kind of relationship the only interaction you have is based on where you should invest your chunk of money, and you don't talk with him or her again until you have more money to invest, or need to move something from one investment to another.

That's what stockbrokers do. That's what insurance salesmen do, and, for that matter, that's also what many financial advisors do. The distinction is that those people are trained to look at whether the recommendations they make for you are suitable for your *needs at the moment*. That recommendation may ultimately be in your best interests or not, but for these professionals, the question is, is it an appropriate investment vehicle for you right now? Initially, he or she will do some sort of risk tolerance analysis to evaluate how much risk can you tolerate. But the fact that you are willing to risk losing 20, 30, 40, or 50 percent doesn't mean you should because if you don't need to take the risk, why in the world would you?

Even so, a stockbroker or an insurance salesman is going to tell you that you can afford to take X level of risk and is then going to sell you something commensurate with the risk that he figured you could take. He might have put you in nothing but high-tech stocks in 2000 when you were getting ready to retire in a year because you thought you could withstand ups and downs in the market. But if he made that investment choice for you in 2000, you lost 20 percent that year, and another 25 percent in 2001, and another 20 percent in 2002, and suddenly, you're not feeling so aggressive after all, are you? The fact is that you should never have taken that risk in the first place if you were retiring in 2000. But that's what brokers and salespeople do. They don't really look at the big picture, and they don't take a holistic approach to the planning process. They're focused on where to put your money in order to grow it. They might do a great job. They might do a poor job. They might do an average job, but their emphasis is on where and how to invest your money today.

For a financial planner, where the money is invested and how it's allocated are important factors and pieces of the overall puzzle, but they're not the be-all and end-all. Where the money's invested is important, certainly, but the bigger picture for me is crafting a strategy that allows you to take a safe, steady, reliable and predictable income stream from that money, an income stream that you and your spouse won't outlive. It's not how much money you make along the way. It's how much money you have to spend along the way. At the end of the day, how much you make matters less than how much you keep.

A financial planner is going to look at the income stream. How are you going to take money out tax-efficiently? The financial planner is going to look at protecting and preserving it. This has to do with the notion of moving from the accumulation phase of life, which is what financial advisors and stockbrokers and insurance salesmen talk to you about, to the preservation and distribution phase of life, which is what a planner will guide you through. A good planner will look at the tax efficiency of your plan and will talk to you about all the other considerations I've covered in this book. He's going to talk to you about estate planning issues. What does your will look like? What do your powers of attorney look like? Have you established a legacy plan? What does retirement look like to you in general? A financial planner is going to go beyond the scope of simply where to invest the money. It really has to do with looking at the entire picture to make sure all the pieces of the puzzle are fitting together. Basically, if there's a dollar sign involved in the decision, you should be having a discussion with a financial planner about it, because that's what his or her expertise is.

Let's talk a moment here about the idea of fiduciary duty. As I mentioned, the jobs of a financial advisor, a stockbroker, an insurance salesman, and a financial salesman are about making sure that whatever investment recommendation they make to you is suitable at the time, but they don't have a fiduciary duty toward you. They don't take into account the multiple factors that make your situation unique. They're not going to ask about any obligations you might have to help support your parents, for instance, and they're not going to talk about your commitment to your children or grandchildren. All they do is make sure that the investment they're endorsing is suitable right now.

By contrast, financial planners have a fiduciary duty to you, which is a higher standard. They have to make sure that what they're doing is in *your best interest,* not just suitable, and there's often a distinct difference between those two things.

There was a good example of this during the mid-1990s into the mid-2000s, when hundreds of thousands of retirees – people in their seventies and eighties – were being sold index annuities by insurance salesmen. Is an index annuity suitable for a seventy- to eighty-year-old? Yes, it's suitable because you're not going to lose any of your money, and if the stock market goes up you might get some percentage of the stock market's gains. However, the question shouldn't be whether it's suitable, but rather, whether it is in your best interest. In the 1990s and for most of the last two decades, I would argue that index annuities were not suitable for most people because, up until two or three years ago, most did not allow you to walk away with your principal. You had to take 5 or 10 percent out over your lifetime, and when you died, your spouse had to take 5 or 10 percent out over his or her lifetime. Then when your spouse died, your children took 5 or 10 percent out until the whole thing was depleted. There was never a walk-away feature. How can a product that doesn't allow you to walk away with your money ever be in your best interest? I just don't think that it is, and that's the difference between having a suitability obligation and having a fiduciary obligation.

From my perspective, you want to work with somebody who puts your interests first and discloses all the strings attached including any conflicts of interest. That's what financial planners will do for you. They'll tell you the pros and cons of any type of investment vehicles or any type of legacy planning or any type of estate planning. It's their job to show you both sides of the question along with any strings attached so that you're sufficiently well informed to make a rational decision on your plan. Some of the topics you'll need to discuss are fairly convoluted and complex, and a good financial planner will take three or four meetings or as many as you need to insure that you have a thorough understanding of them. That understanding creates a comfort level for you in knowing exactly where you stand in terms of your retirement. Remember, I said earlier that my clients want a simple verifiable plan. That is what a good planner will do for you.

So how do you go about choosing a financial planner, and what should you look for? Certainly, education comes into play. Can a retired police officer be a fantastic financial planner? Absolutely. Can somebody with a master's degree in finance be a horrible financial planner? Absolutely. So although education is important, it's not the only thing that you need to weigh. The same thing is true about certification. Just because someone has a certified financial planner designation doesn't mean that he or she is a good financial planner, any more than having a law degree means someone is a good attorney. In choosing your financial planner, take the time to sit down with him before you hire him and get a feel for the way he thinks.

Do his monetary and investment philosophies match what you're looking for? Does he meet your expectations? Is he in sync with where you are, emotionally and mentally, regarding money? If not, he's not the right planner for you. It doesn't mean that he's a bad planner, it just means he's not the right planner for you.

Additionally, I certainly think you want to look at his education. You want to be sure that his education is ongoing and you want to look at his years of experience. It's so easy to get licensed in this industry and never take another class, to omit the type of continuing education that's required to keep abreast of the newest information or the newest strategies. What type of economic services does she subscribe to? What type of analysis does he get? Who are they getting their training from? How often are they getting training? All those things are reasonable to expect and those are things that you should look for when you're talking to a financial planner.

As far as what you should expect, I think most planners anticipate conversation with their clients from both sides of the table because this is a working relationship that ideally should be designed to last a lifetime. It's not something that you want to bounce in and out of. It's a little like getting married because you do get very personally involved with your financial planner. You become members of each other's extended families in that a good financial planner has to truly understand the dynamics of your family in order to make good, sound recommendations.

Services You Should Expect From Your Advisor

QUARTERLY AND YEARLY INVESTMENT REVIEWS

We take a look at your investments and have a conversation about current and future allocations. We talk about goals. Are your investments still meeting your financial goals? We make changes when appropriate and in response to your input.

GOAL SETTING AND STATUS UPDATES

We have a candid conversation about your financial and professional goals. We provide a plan that will help you accomplish those goals. We help you stay on track and keep your goals in sight.

RETIREMENT PLANNING

Whether you are in retirement or still saving for retirement, we provide analysis that will give you an idea whether or not you are on pace to hit your goals. This analysis provides information that will give you a better understanding of whether or not you will be able to retire with the amount of income you want or if you will be able to sustain your current retirement income through your retirement. It will also provide alternative solutions if there are any shortcomings.

ASSET ALLOCATION ANALYSIS

We go through a series of questions that assesses your risk tolerance. We provide an analysis of what your risk tolerance is in regards to the market and your investments. We have a conversation about your risk tolerance and how that can help you reach your financial goals. We take the approach that once your goals are set, risk should be adjusted accordingly.

RETIREMENT PLAN ANALYSIS

For those individuals who currently have a retirement plan through their employer. We analyze and make recommendations on the funds you should be invested in, according to your asset allocation analysis and risk tolerance.

HOMEOWNERS AND AUTO INSURANCE ANALYSIS

We do an analysis of your homeowners and auto insurance. We do not sell those lines of insurance. However, we make sure you are properly insured with the correct limits. Frequently, we find clients are underinsured and we find alternative ways to save you money.

LONG TERM CARE AND DISABILITY INSURANCE ANALYSIS

We do an analysis of any currently held long-term care or disability policies. We talk about how these types of policies can fit into your financial plan. We discuss the legacy planning aspects of protecting your heirs and loved ones.

LIFE AND HEALTH INSURANCE ANALYSIS

We do an analysis of life and health insurance policies. We assist in the selection of gap coverage for retirees as well as making sure working clients obtain the protection they need from their health insurance policies. We also examine what type of life insurance you should own, if any. In addition, we examine life insurance as a legacy and tax planning tool.

ESTATE PLANNING AND ANALYSIS

We review all of your current estate planning documents: your wills, powers of attorney, medical care directives, living wills, and trust documents. We make sure you have the correct language needed and your wills and powers of attorney are up to date. If there are no estate planning documents in place, we go through a series of questions that provide an attorney a much more thorough understanding of what you and your family require.

TAX PROJECTIONS ANALYSIS

We review the last three years of your tax returns. We analyze your current situation and project any changes you can make to save you tax dollars. We also make sure you have funds set up in the correct accounts to insure that when it comes time to start withdrawing those funds, you can take them out in the most tax-efficient matter. After all, it isn't how much you make. It is how much you keep.

CASH MANAGEMENT ANALYSIS

If you are a client who is in distribution mode – typically retirees – we do an analysis of your investments and come up with a tax-efficient strategy to identify the best place from which to take your distributions. We also have conversations about how your cash flows. Do we need to take more or less? If you are a client who is in savings mode, we take a look at your income versus your budget and try to find ways to maximize your savings.

EDUCATION PLANNING AND ANALYSIS

If you have children or grandchildren for whose education you would like to start saving, we will do an analysis of where the savings should come from and where it should be invested. There are a number of different vehicles that can be used for education purposes and a number of different investments to choose from. We will devise the most cost- and tax-effective strategy to invest for your loved ones' futures.

MORTGAGE ANALYSIS

For many clients, there are numerous questions when it comes to buying or selling a home: whether or not to refinance, or how different mortgage programs like reverse mortgages work. We can help answer your questions and provide you with analysis and illustrations on future or current scenarios.

IRA, PENSION, RETIREMENT DISTRIBUTIONS

There are tax-efficient ways to take money out of your retirement accounts, paying the least amount of taxes possible. We find that many taxpayers lose more to taxes than they should because of the way they take their distributions from their retirement accounts. We help our clients save thousands of dollars by helping them withdraw their funds in the most tax-efficient manner.

You want to have a conversation about your expectations and your financial planner's expectations: How often are we going to meet? How are you going to communicate with me? What rates of return should I expect? Who on your staff should I be dealing with on a regular basis? Are you the only person I work with? What happens if something happens to you? Those are all reasonable questions to which you should get clear answers. Whatever you're expecting from the relationship, you surely should make that clear. There may be expectations that he or she is not willing to meet or can't meet for various reasons, but you should always set forth the expectations that you have and, conversely, financial planners should tell you what their expectations are of you.

For example, in our practice we expect you to come to our meetings prepared and on time just as you should expect me to be at our meetings prepared and on time. The first Tuesday of every quarter we hold an economic review at which we sit down with all the clients and talk about what's going on in the market, the trends we see, and why we think the economy's going in certain directions, and we expect you, as our client, to attend one or two of these a year. We don't need you there every time, but my expectation is that you will do your part in staying informed by attending. If your statement comes in and something doesn't make sense, I expect you to pick up the phone and make a call to me. I expect you to tell me when things change in your life, so I don't have to guess what's going on. I expect you to embrace our philosophy and the direction in which we go. I expect you to want to verify and see in simple writing what we're doing and how we're doing, but if you agree to implement the direction, I expect you to honor your word because I'm doing what I said I was going to do, and you need to do what you said you were going to do. Those expectations are laid out in advance because nobody likes surprises.

It's a two-way street. There's a list of questions that are reasonable to ask the financial planner, the financial advisor, the stockbroker, or the insurance salesman.

How to be certain you find and hire the best advisor for *your* unique goals

Seven Sure-Fire Steps to Hiring the Best Advisor

STEP 1
DON'T GO IT ALONE!

The rules of the game are changing rapidly today. You need knowledgeable and experienced guides who focus on solving these types of financial and legal problems. These guides won't be found in the form of your favorite bank teller, nor at the local coffee shop, beauty salon, or golf course.

The greatest protection available will be with specialized teams of professionals who have both a qualified elder-law attorney and an advisor who specializes in asset protection.

STEP 2
IF IT SOUNDS TOO GOOD TO BE TRUE, IT PROBABLY IS.

It's a common and scary trend today to hear seniors who have made poor decisions based on "buying into great opportunities." For instance, if a financial salesperson tells you about a 9 percent CD when you know darn well the bank down the road is paying 1.25 percent on CDs, guess what? That's a red flag, a giant, waving red flag. When you hear something that sounds good and you want to believe it, ask the person this simple question, so what are the strings attached? If they say "no strings," then you need to turn and run. There are a lot of great financial products with attractive features, but even the great opportunities out there come with "rules" (aka, strings attached). You need to know what they are and if they are acceptable to you and in line with your planning goals. Always use and trust your own good judgment and common sense.

STEP 3
BEWARE OF "FREE." THERE IS NO FREE LUNCH.

Marketers use bait-and-switch techniques on retirees constantly. Let me outline a few that we are very wary of. First, let's dissect the free lunch or dinner seminar offer. Obviously, when you get an invitation saying, "Hey, I'll buy you dinner – no worries. Nothing is ever sold," your good old common sense should kick in and say, "This person is going to do something to get my money" – red flag. I'm certainly not saying you shouldn't go to seminars to learn. We do monthly seminars, but our newspaper insert invites people to come and learn, not to eat a free steak dinner. Also be careful of organizations that say they help veterans get benefits for "free." In reality, these are financial salesmen. You can only get help with VA matters from a veteran service organization (like the VFW), an accredited agent, or a certified lawyer. Again, "free" here ends up costing you money.

STEP 4
WATCH OUT FOR LEGAL ADVICE FROM NONLAWYERS.

We know the value of integrating trust documentation and specific financial products. However, be very cautious when the purchase of a financial product also entitles you to free legal documents to support the plan. This is where you can be penny-wise and fortune- foolish. Our business model at Prostatis is designed for collaboration among like-minded professionals focused on meeting the goals and objectives of the client. No one professional can wear all of these hats and be good at all of these jobs. A key defense of having your money snatched is to realize legal documents cost money, and a packaged offer with legal documentation included (based on the purchase of a product) should be a giant red flag.

STEP 5
BEWARE OF ONLINE "RESOURCES."

Information online should be viewed with a very skeptical eye. Today it is not uncommon for retirees to jump online to do "research." The critical question is, are you getting information from a credible source? This can be very difficult to decipher online. Information overload is another problem. If you enter the keyword "revocable trust" on Google, you'll come up with about 962,000 articles, websites, and "resources" to look at. The problem is, before you've finished looking at 962,000 online "resources," you'd be dead and your family would be burdened by the cost and time delay of probate. (Obviously this would defeat your original planning goal.)

Yes, you need to do research but on the right thing: Finding the right help. Focus your due diligence on finding the right planning team to assist you (as we discussed in step one).

STEP 6
DEMAND PROOF!

There's nothing worse than being sold a bad idea. Slick talk can be very persuasive, but it may prove financially disastrous. When seeking professional advice, we recommend that you assess just how accomplished your potential advice-giver really is. How that person answers the following questions should give you a good idea of his or her qualifications and passion for the work.

Have you ever been published in an industry periodical?
Industry magazines are looking for real experts because they want their readers to get credible and accurate information. Both you and the publication need someone who doesn't just talk a good game, but someone who really knows his or her stuff.

Are you an author on this subject?
Professionals who take time to write have a passion for what they do. They've taken time to spell out their planning methods and beliefs. It's not easy writing a book, so they are dedicated and serious about their profession and proud of what they do. Plus, you'll be able to obtain their book, read it, and then check that the advice that they are giving you is in line with the message they published in their book.

Do you invest in your professional knowledge?
This question is a great way to gauge the prospective advisor's commitment to staying current on new laws, tax code changes, and cutting edge ideas to help preserve and grow your wealth.

The same goes for lawyers. If you have a large IRA, you might be swayed knowing an advisor has trained with Ed Slott, a recognized expert CPA in the area of IRA planning. Likewise, a multidisciplinary lawyer who invests nearly $24,000 a year to belong to an elite advisor coaching group is certainly educated on the latest and most effective long-term care planning strategies available to preserve and protect his or her clients' life savings.

Which professionals refer business to you?

It's common to ask for references, but I believe this is a loaded proposition. It wouldn't be too hard to find three or four people who like an advisor or lawyer and would give that person a good reference. Our question is much different. A number of healthcare facilities refer to us because they know we help their patients pay for care and help their families. That certainly means more than just having a friend or client say nice things about us. The professional referral source has zero incentive to give false praise. To them it's all about how well we get the job done. This is a much more credible source of information to assess just how good an advisor or lawyer is at his or her craft. Again, truly effective planning advice comes from well-organized teams of professionals, which is logical since no one person can be good at all things.

STEP 7
BE SMART AND TRUST YOUR FEELINGS.

Much is revealed when you meet face to face. See how you feel. We believe that every person who walks through our doors needs to be treated as if they are a member of our own family. We invite you to come meet us and see if you feel comfortable and more secure about your future. There's no cost or obligation to become a client after our Complete Planning Review (CPR).

Now, keep in mind, not everybody's going to give the same answer, and not everybody's going to have the ideal answer, and remember that it is a two-way street. A salesman – a stockbroker, an advisor, an insurance salesman – is going to do whatever he needs to do in order to sell you a product because he gets paid for selling you a product.

But with financial planners, it's an interview on both sides. Financial planners will take on people who fit the style of practice that they have, and you should only work with a financial planner with whom you fit. I know from our perspective that we work well with certain types of people. I am not the right fit for everybody, and any financial planner who thinks that he is the right fit for everybody is not a financial planner, he's a financial salesman, and you want to distinguish that because you don't want to be with a financial salesman. You want to be with somebody who's going to plan with your best interests in mind.

I think two of the questions that are always worrisome for people are, first, what are the strings attached? And second, how does this person get paid? These are certainly questions that you always want to ask because there a lot of different ways that advisors, financial planners, stockbrokers, or insurance salesmen get paid.

Salesmen get paid on a transaction basis. That means they're getting a commission. Sometimes when a stockbroker buys and sells a stock, he charges a fee to do so. It might be a couple of hundred bucks per transaction, which means that in order for him to make a living, he has to conduct many transactions. He's going to conduct them with you or conduct them with somebody, but the way he gets paid is on those commissions. That always raises the question of whether he's putting his interests ahead of yours or yours ahead of his, which is why we prefer planners.

The same thing holds true for financial advisors, investment salesmen, and insurance salesmen: They all sell products that carry a commission. There are mutual funds that pay commissions, and there are annuities that pay commissions, and the problem is that it sometimes raises a conflict. Is he or she making that mutual fund recommendation because it is the best mutual fund out there for you or because it's paying a 5 percent commission? The same issue arises with an annuity. Is he or she making the recommendation because it's the best annuity for you or because it's paying somewhere between a 3 and a 10 percent commission?

There is nothing wrong with having a relationship with somebody who generates revenue on a commission because quite frankly most insurance products pay a commission of some sort, but you have to be careful about the underlying motive for selling that particular commissionable product. If it fits into a well-laid-out plan, then it's absolutely fine to pay an advisor some sort of a commission to provide that particular product for you. The problem is that short-term advisors are not planning. They're selling you a product in a vacuum just because it's suitable right now. It's not because it's in your best interest, or because it fits into an overall plan, which is our concern.

Conversely, from our perspective, it's not that financial planners won't use an investment vehicle that generates a commission, but they will tell you how they get paid, up front. They never tell you, "Don't worry about my fees, I get paid by somebody else," or "They pay me to bring you to the table." Any time you hear somebody say, "Don't worry about my fees," you should worry about the fees because it means that you're not going to see the fees, and therefore you're not going to know what the fees are. It's not that it's necessarily a bad thing, but you know what? You should know what you're paying and what services you're getting.

With a fee-based financial planner, you're going to see your fees. A fee-based financial planner is going to tell you, "I charge by the hour. Here's how many hours I think it's going to take for me to create your plan, so this is the bill you should expect." A fee-based financial planner might also charge a flat fee, based on the amount of time he or she expects it will take to create your plan on an ongoing basis over the course of the year. A fee-based financial planner typically will charge a fee based on the assets under management that he's actually controlling. So, for a family that comes to him with a house worth $250,000 and $500,000 worth of retirement accounts, he is going to charge 1 percent, 2 percent – whatever the number is that you've agreed to – on the $500,000 that he is managing for you. If he puts some of that money into an annuity because it pays a commission, he's not going to charge you a fee on the money that he puts into the annuity. Let's say, for example, the plan includes using

$250,000 of your money to provide an income stream. He's going to buy two separate annuities to fund your retirement income buckets. That leaves $250,000 in money that he's managing. He's going to charge you a fee on that $250,000, but because he probably got paid a commission for putting your money into these annuities, he's not going charge you a fee on those.

You always want to understand how they get paid. It's not necessarily an issue of how much they're getting paid. You just want to know how they're making their money so you'll understand why they're selling you the products they're selling you. Knowing how they get paid takes that potential conflict off the table.

I've included a list of things to watch out for when you're interviewing a potential planner or advisor. Personally, I'd shy away from anybody who wants to close the business on the first date. These are important decisions. You need time to think about it. It doesn't mean that the person is necessarily doing anything wrong. I just think if anybody shows up and says, "You need to do this today and if you don't, bad things are going happen to you," that's the type of relationship you walk away from.

If somebody doesn't tell you up front how much time he's locking your money up for or doesn't make clear the time commitment you're going to have for these various buckets of money, to me, that's a problem. You want to make sure that your advisor explains all the strings attached to your investments. To me, it raises a red flag when somebody comes to your house for initial meetings unless you are incapacitated for some reason. You need to go see where the person works. It shouldn't be, "I'll meet you in a coffee shop." It's not that somebody can't have a viable practice out of his basement. I just worry about what type of background and education or service that you can expect if that person is working out of the basement.

A home office is a different thing. Your potential planner should have a place where you can go look and get a feel for what the office is like. When you show up in his or her office, if it doesn't look professional, it's probably not professional. I recognize that certified public accountants who read this might be offended because we all know that when you walk into CPAs' offices, they have piles of paper everywhere. To me, that visible lack of organization is a red flag. You don't want your retirement in a disorganized mess. I think you also want to be careful about advisors who bounce around from firm to firm to firm. Don't be afraid to ask them how long they've been with that firm, and what the transition plan is if they should leave.

I'm always asked if I have had complaints lodged against me. Yes, you can go to Broker Check at the FINRA website to find out if there are complaints about someone. While it is important to look at the complaints, you need to do so in light of the fact that we're a very litigious society, and every day there's a commercial on TV that tells you to sue your advisor. Even though there's a complaint, it doesn't necessarily mean that there's a problem with that broker or that advisor or that planner. And the same thing holds true for the firm that they work with. Just because there has been a complaint or there's some negative publicity about the firm, remember that one bad apple doesn't ruin the whole batch.

Going back to the conversation in which you're interviewing a potential planner, assuming that you've done your homework and your research, these are some of the questions you might want to ask:

- Why is your office such a mess?
- We were supposed to meet at three and you didn't get in to see me until three twenty. Is this a normal pattern?
- How do you get paid?
- Do I work with you or a member of your staff?

- How often do we meet?
- How quickly do you return phone calls?

These are but a few questions you might ask. The most important thing is that you should ask questions to make sure you are on the same page with your advisor.

CONCLUSION

CONCLUSION

What I've tried to do for you in this book is to provide you with a reasonable plan of attack to address your retirement needs. The information we've provided here is applicable to somebody who's going into retirement within the next ten years, but also to somebody who's in retirement now and doesn't feel that it's working out the way he or she thought it would. It's also meant to be helpful to somebody who just wants a good second opinion. The information that we've provided here could be very beneficial for anybody, regardless of whether he or she anticipates hiring a planner or plans to do his or her own retirement planning. We have the charts and we have the information so that you can create your own, sound, financial plan to create a safe, predictable, reliable, and steady income stream for you and your spouse. I hope you'll take the opportunity to visit my website, www.prostatisfinancial.com, and take advantage of those resources.

The fact is that most folks do more research on which washing machine to buy than they do on income planning for that twenty to thirty years of retirement. I hope this book has fine-tuned that for you, put it into perspective, and broken it down into pieces that are easy to digest so that you too can take a step-by-step approach to your retirement planning. We've tried to provide you with relevant information that leads to a more successful, happier, and less stressful retirement because going through retirement should not result in sleepless nights.

CPSIA information can be obtained at www.ICGtesting.com
Printed in the USA
BVOW04s1631050314

346769BV00007B/64/P